Praise for

"Wealth-related magic has [...] should you or shouldn't you?* Pamela Chen says *should* and encourages you to practice it without shame. Within the first few chapters, she'll convince you that you can have anything you want in life—because you can. Filled with easy-to-follow spells, richuals, and personal anecdotes, you'll feel like you're on top of the world after an encouraging heart-to-heart with your money savvy witch bestie!"

—**AMANDA LOVELACE**, author of *Make Your Own Magic*

"Are you ready to manifest your most prosperous life? In Pamela Chen's newest book, *Wealth Witchery*, she guides you on creating a successful wealth practice and exactly what tools, mindset, and steps are needed to help make that happen. With the included easy-to-do spells and 'richuals,' you can create a comprehensive plan to increase your abundance. I love the lucky frog richual and will be trying that soon."

—**JEN SANKEY**, author/creator of *Enchanted Forest Felines Tarot* and *Stardust Wanderer Tarot*

"Enter the enchanting realm of *Wealth Witchery* with Pamela's expert guidance. These practices have transformed my personal mindset, energy, and relationship with money. A must-read for those ready to unlock their inner power and manifest true prosperity with these proven tools that have yielded instant results for me and others!"

—**KELLEY KNIGHT**, author of *Spells for the Modern Mystic*

"*Wealth Witchery* turns the path to financial abundance into an exciting and fun adventure. Blending magical practices with practical tips, this book makes manifesting money a joyful and enchanting experience. Filled with engaging exercises and Chen's inspiring personal stories, *Wealth Witchery* is perfect for anyone looking to bring a little more prosperity into their life. You'll transform your relationship with money and learn to harness it as a powerful, dynamic energy!"

—**MAT AURYN,** author of *Psychic Witch, Mastering Magick,* and *The Psychic Art of Tarot*

"The perfect read for those looking to harness the power of witchcraft for financial abundance. For beginner witches to seasoned practitioners and those in between, *Wealth Witchery* offers insightful wisdom empowering the reader shift belief systems around money, abundance, and success. Easy-to-read and packed with powerful tips, *Wealth Witchery* is your gateway to wealth magic."

—**SAM MAGDALENO,** author of *The Big Book of Tarot Meanings* and *The Tarot Spellbook*

WEALTH
WITCHERY

About the Author

Pamela Chen is the author of *Enchanted Crystal Magic* and creator of *Witchling Academy Tarot* and *Tarot of the Owls*. She also works as a business, wealth, and money manifesting coach. She helps spiritual entrepreneurs become more than just a "tarot reader" and trains the next generation of coaches and healers to become energetic mas-ters. When she is not writing or coaching, she loves to cuddle with her chickens, watch Korean drama, and eat spicy Cheeto puffs with avocado. Visit her at MagicalPam.com.

To Write to the Author

If you wish to contact the author or would like more information about this book, please write to the author in care of Llewellyn Worldwide Ltd. and we will forward your request. Both the author and publisher appreciate hearing from you and learning of your enjoyment of this book and how it has helped you. Llewellyn Worldwide Ltd. cannot guarantee that every letter written to the author can be answered, but all will be forwarded. Please write to:

Pamela Chen
℅ Llewellyn Worldwide
2143 Wooddale Drive
Woodbury, MN 55125-2989
Please enclose a self-addressed stamped envelope for reply,
or $1.00 to cover costs. If outside the U.S.A., enclose
an international postal reply coupon.

Many of Llewellyn's authors have websites with additional information and resources. For more information, please visit our website at http://www.llewellyn.com.

WEALTH WITCHERY

MANIFESTING MAGIC, MONEY, AND SUCCESS

PAMELA CHEN

LLEWELLYN
WOODBURY, MINNESOTA

FIRST EDITION
First Printing, 2025

Book design by Samantha Peterson
Cover design by Kevin R. Brown
Interior illustrations by Llewellyn Art Department

Llewellyn Publications is a registered trademark of Llewellyn Worldwide Ltd.

Library of Congress Cataloging-in-Publication Data
Names: Chen, Pamela, author.
Title: Wealth witchery : manifesting magic, money, and success / by Pamela Chen.
Description: First edition. | Woodbury, MN : Llewellyn Publications, a Division of Llewellyn Worldwide Ltd, [2025] | Summary: "With simple daily and weekly practices, Wealth Witchery offers the magical boost every go-getter needs to live their best life" —Provided by publisher.
Identifiers: LCCN 2024057461 (print) | LCCN 2024057462 (ebook) | ISBN 9780738773537 (paperback) | ISBN 9780738773629 (ebook)
Subjects: LCSH: Witchcraft. | Witches. | Magic.
Classification: LCC BF1566 .C4784 2025 (print) | LCC BF1566 (ebook) | DDC 203/.3—dc23/eng/20250106
LC record available at https://lccn.loc.gov/2024057461
LC ebook record available at https://lccn.loc.gov/2024057462

Llewellyn Publications
A Division of Llewellyn Worldwide Ltd.
2143 Wooddale Drive
Woodbury, MN 55125-2989
www.llewellyn.com

Printed in the United States of America

Other Books by Pamela Chen

Caticorn Tarot
Crystal Unicorn Tarot
Enchanted Crystal Magic
Galactic Star Tarot
The Mandarin Tree
Steampunk Faerie Tarot
Tarot of the Owls
Witchling Academy Tarot

This book is dedicated to all my family, friends, and mentors who have helped and supported me through my wealth journey. Thank you for all the borrowed money and treating me to yummy food.

CONTENTS

List of Spells and Richuals · xi

Disclaimer · xiii

Foreword by Silver RavenWolf · xv

Introduction · 1

One: Money + Magic + Wealth Witchery · 9

Two: Wealth Witchery Tools · 19

Three: Abundance Altars · 45

Four: Your Wealth Witchery Practice · 61

Five: Level Up Your Relationship with Money · 85

Six: Prosperity Dream Board · 101

Seven: Rich Witch Soul Essence · 115

Eight: Writing Your Rich Reality · 127

Contents

Nine: Wealth Witchery Spells · 143

Ten: Richuals Throughout the Year · 177

Eleven: What's Next? · 217

Conclusion · 223

SPELLS AND RICHUALS

Spells

Instant Cash Spell • 144

Lucky Prosperity Spell • 146

Open Roads to Opportunity Spell • 149

Wealthy Me Spell • 152

Rich Business Charm Spell • 156

Fame and Fortune Spell • 158

Millionaire Money Spell • 160

Client Attraction Spell • 162

Winning Money Spell • 165

Simmer Pot Prosperity Spell • 168

Stepping Through the Abundance Portal Spell • 171

Bling-Bling Spell • 173

Green Salt Money Spell • 207

Richuals

New Moon Money Richual • 178

Full Moon Money Richual • 181

Mercury Retrograde Richual • 185

New Year's Richual • 188

Honoring the Year Coming to an End Richual • 191

Monday Money Richual • 194

Birthday Wish Richual • 198

Dressing For Success Richual • 200

Lucky Money Shower Richual • 202

Green Salt Crafting Richual • 204

Prosperity Frog Richual • 209

Morning Quantum Portal Richual • 210

11:11 Richual • 213

DISCLAIMER

The information in this book is provided for educational and informational purposes only. Such information is not a substitute nor replacement for advice, diagnosis, or treatment from a licensed mental health or medical professional. The author and publisher encourage you to consult a professional if you have questions about the use or efficacy of any of the techniques or insights in this book. In the following pages you will find recommendations for the use of certain herbs, essential oils, anointing oils, and magical tools. Each body reacts differently to herbs, essential oils, and other items, so results may vary person to person. If you are allergic to any of these items, please refrain from use. Essential oils are potent; use care when handling them, and always dilute them with a carrier oil.

Finally, practice fire safety by keeping a close eye on an open flame. Never leave a lit flame unattended.

FOREWORD

In *Wealth Witchery: Manifesting Magic, Money, and Success*, Pamela Chen offers a luminous guide that seamlessly blends the mystical with the practical. As an online entrepreneur with a modern-day rags-to-riches story, Pamela's enthusiasm and bright spirit shine through every page, inspiring readers to embrace their "rich witch soul essence" and transform their financial reality.

Drawing from her journey, Pamela provides an array of powerful tools and practices, from setting up a prosperity altar to creating a Prosperity Dream Board. She shares spells, workings, and monthly and yearly rituals designed to align your intentions with the abundant energies of the universe. With her practical manifestation strategies, you'll learn how to give, spend, and receive money in ways that will transform your relationship with wealth in a dynamic and exciting way.

Pamela's approach is grounded and empowering, showing that we can only manifest what we truly believe. Through her sincere guidance, you'll discover how to channel your desires into tangible results, cultivating a life of magic, money, and success. Wealth Witchery is not just a book; it's an invitation to reimagine your financial destiny with the wisdom of a seasoned coach and the heart of a true believer. Let Pamela Chen's vibrant and sincere teachings guide you to a prosperous future where every day is a spell for success.

—Silver RavenWolf

INTRODUCTION

For as long as I can remember, I've been studying, practicing, and using magic to manifest money. When people tell me money cannot buy you happiness, I shake my head. It's true having money cannot guarantee happiness, but it can make your life easier and enable you to pay for the experiences and resources that make you happy. The key is not to place all your focus on the money itself, even though that is a part of it. What is most important is to put your energy toward creating overall wealth and abundance in all areas of your life. Creating that powerful and transformational life experience is the intention of *Wealth Witchery*.

I can absolutely tell you things were much harder when I didn't have money. There were times when I was worried about paying rent and had to decide whether or not I could even afford toothpaste. Before we dive deeper into the practice of wealth witchery and all the magic contained within this book, I would like to share my own story, including how I began using magic to manifest money and the amazing opportunities that have continued to flow into my life since. If you look at my Instagram profile right now, you might think, *She already has it all, so of course manifesting money is easy.* I've had people tell me this. However, after reading my story, you will see that anyone at any time can manifest more prosperity and money into their bank account, regardless of their past or current circumstances.

Money was a struggle for me in the early years of my life. My family lived in Hawaii, and when I was around sixteen years old, they planned to move across the island. I decided to move out because I wanted to stay close to school. Luckily, I had a friend whose aunt gave us an amazing deal on a house to rent. To pay my rent, I worked a part-time job while going to high school. At that time, part-time pay was only five dollars an hour, so that didn't get me very far. However, I am naturally a pretty optimistic and high-achieving person, so I went out and got better jobs to make more money. Living in Hawaii is quite expensive, so I had to get creative. Then, my friend and I had to move, and our next place had higher rent. I ended up living in a three-bedroom apartment with seven people and sharing a room with my best friend. I was working to make as much money as I could. In a way, it was fun to live paycheck-to-paycheck at that time, since I was partying every night with no responsibilities. But it grew old. I knew there was something more I wanted to accomplish, but I had no idea what.

I became obsessed with going to see psychics. I know now that I was drawn to psychics because I was actually seeking my own spirituality; I was interested in magic. Back in 2003, there weren't online courses or social media events that provided this type of information or insight. Through the many psychic readings I received, I found my first magical mentor, and she taught me and my friends our first money spell. She taught us other things too, such as how to meditate, visualize, astral travel, and work with angels, though I was most drawn to money magic.

After practicing some of the money magic the psychic taught me, I started to have better luck with money. For example, my car broke down, and the exact amount of money I needed to repair it came the next week from a former employer that had "forgotten" to give me my last paycheck. Then, I was able to pay off a $10,000 gambling debt I had incurred previously, in part because I was gifted money. Many, many more money miracles started to happen in my life.

A few years later, after taking courses and classes on various ways to work with magic, manifesting, and energy work, I ended up in Las Vegas, Nevada. Boy, did the money flow in after I moved there! I started out making six figures with full-time benefits—without a college degree—as a dealer in a casino on the Strip. However, even though I had achieved my goal of making a lot of money, I still felt like something was missing.

Do you ever feel like you are meant to live another life, like there is something more than your current life experience? That was how I felt. So, I kept searching and focused my intentions on creating something more. Doing this resulted in me getting to know myself on a deeper level. I explored my creativity, insight, and talent, and I started to expand in new ways. I felt inspired and began taking chances, which resulted in me creating my first tarot deck.

That deck led to my first publishing contract and opening up an online crystal boutique. As I continued to stay open to expansion, more and more opportunities began to present themselves. This included one of my next major steps, which was to become an online entrepreneur providing coaching in crystal magic and deck creation. Everything slowly came together from there, with the biggest shift happening in 2020 when I was able to quit my job at the casino, where I had worked for thirteen years, to do what I loved most full-time. Now, I generate six figures every year via my ever-expanding coaching business, and I have published six tarot decks, one oracle deck, and three books! Wow, can you believe it? Me, someone who was not brought up learning about how to create a successful business or an abundance of money, and who didn't even write an essay in school! I have accomplished all of these things, and you can too!

The magic and manifestation techniques that I am sharing in this book were developed through fifteen-plus years of learning. I continually manifested what I most wanted to create in my life, which included financial wealth and success. If I can do it, I believe anyone can. You truly can manifest anything you want if you commit to developing your magical practice, use the tools, and stay open to opportunities when they present themselves to you.

This is not a book about how to invest in stocks, balance your bank account, or run a business. Instead, in this book I share the energetic and metaphysical side of attaining abundance and wealth. You will learn how to open the door to prosperity using practical magic, how to create a money mindset, and how to attune your energy to attract more money and opportunities into your life. I do suggest pairing this book with physical action; find a mentor or coach who can offer money strategies and advice. Your magic will need some kind of action to fuel it as well as a structure for creation.

Although it took me over a decade to manifest my rich witch life, reading this book could make it happen faster for you. I'm sharing the process and manifestation system I developed over the years so you don't have to figure it all out for yourself! This is the reason I wrote this book: I intend to bring these successful practices—and the magic associated with them—into the mainstream. I enjoy my life so much, and I want to help others live their dream too.

If you are reading this book, there is a reason why. It is most likely that deep in your soul, you have a desire for more in your life.

You want to have, do, or be more than you are now, though what that means will be unique for you. Being abundant looks different for everyone, and you can change your goals at any time. Perhaps you want to create something new, live in a new house, go on a dream vacation, sit first class, send your kids to private school, fill up your refrigerator with fresh fruits and vegetables, or manifest a new kitty. Whatever your goal is, all of that and more can be yours.

You might be a witch or an advanced practitioner of magic, or you might just be curious about magic. It's also possible that you want to understand the connection between magic and wealth so you can help others. In fact, you may already know who you would help or donate money to if you were a rich witch. Just for a second, imagine if every healer, witch, amazing human, and heart-centered spiritual entrepreneur was a multi-millionaire. Our world would definitely be a better place. Therefore, it is one of my deepest wishes to help those who have kind intentions and big dreams manifest wealth and prosperity. The truth is, once you receive material manifestations, have financial security, and feel financially supported in life, you can then open the door to a deeper spiritual and magical practice. Being provided for in the material realm could be the first step in your spiritual evolution.

Wherever you are on your journey, this book will help you tap into your money magic. The practical magic and techniques that I share are very easy to follow and can create potent results regardless of your experience level. In this book, you will learn both basic and advanced magical practices for manifesting more money, abundance, and wealth through ascension. The way my magic and my manifestation methods work is through expansion and growth; I do not believe we have to suffer in order to gain riches, nor do I believe we have to sacrifice anything in order to succeed. One of the most powerful beliefs that has served me well is that change can happen quickly and easily.

Since we can only manifest what we believe in, before going any further, make a list of what you believe about manifestation right now. Do you believe that manifestation has to be hard, that you have to suffer before anything good can come to you, or that money is hard to earn? If so, that will become your reality. The truth is, you don't have to stay in that mindset; everything can be easy. Releasing your limiting beliefs is a very important part of this process. Negative beliefs about money and manifestation need to be changed into something positive that will support you on your wealth witchery adventure. I believe the processes and steps I take you through in this book will assist in shifting your belief system, but keep in mind that limiting beliefs must be released at some point for you to consistently create what you want. However, as a first step, being aware of what you believe will already start to change your world. You may begin to notice abundance trickling in just because of this one shift.

To that end, I invite you to read this book chapter by chapter so that you receive the most impactful and magical support as you navigate shifts and create your most desired life. Each chapter builds upon the one before. You might notice that sometimes, the same information is repeated, but in a different way. The purpose of this is to help train the brain to embed these new rich witch beliefs so that you can more easily call money into your life.

Everyone is unique and has different magical gifts and affinities, so some of what works for me might not work for you. Therefore, I do not want you to just blindly follow what I say. It's important for you to become familiar with your own magical self and what does—or does not—work for you. Wealth witchery is just a framework for you to build upon to start manifesting wealth consistently and to discover your own magic. I do suggest you try everything shared in this book at least once. Then, as you become more adept at implementing the practices, modify them as you figure out what resonates with you the most. At first, it can be tricky to determine if something doesn't resonate because you have an affinity for doing it another way, or if it is really resistance showing up because you are being stretched beyond your comfort zone. It's also good to know that if you do experience resistance, this often means abundance is right around the corner.

Chapters 9 and 10 include spells and "richuals" I have created. While you are reading through the book and learning the teachings within it, you can start using them. Try them out! Even young practitioners on a budget can follow the spells and richuals in this book. I designed them to be fun and simple. When I was a teenager trying to learn magic, most spells had so many required tools that I gave up, since I had no money at that time and could not afford to purchase any magical tools. Therefore, the spells and richuals in this book were created with my own experiences in mind. My mission for you, rich witch, is to discover how much you love magical practices (and to be inspired to create your own) without ever being held back by a limited budget or any other obstacle.

One of the most important things I can share to help you be successful is this: Be consistent with your magical craft. Learning to work with enchantment, energy, and manifestation is not a get-rich-quick scheme. Rather, it is a lifelong practice. If you show up and do your magic daily, stay consistent, and focus on what you want, you will have massive results. Reading this today will have already shifted you, so expect a miracle soon.

In my opinion, wealth witchery is one of the best magical practices to learn because if you have wealth and abundance, you will be empowered to live your best life. You will be able to be who you most want to be and do what you most want to do. Always dream big, and know that you can have it all.

Now, let's create some magic!

ONE
MONEY + MAGIC + WEALTH WITCHERY

You've probably heard of witchcraft, which is the study and use of sorcery and magic. Richcraft, also known as wealth witchery, is a niche that I originally created for myself within my magical practices. When I work with magic, 99 percent of the time it is related to the realms of money, fame, and/or business. I love using magic, spells, and rituals to empower my intentions, creating what is desired much more quickly, and now I support others in doing the same.

A couple of years ago, all the spells and rituals that I was creating began to be directed toward money and abundance magic. That's what was important to me at that time. I had a good relationship and was happy in all the other areas of my life. The only thing missing was money and the experiences that come with it, like traveling around the world. For the last few years, I have focused on attracting wealth. That's even what my business was built upon:

helping others manifest money! I never really enjoyed magic regarding relationships, fertility, or other areas of life. However, creating wealth through the practices of wealth witchery is something that I actually really enjoy doing (it's something that I practice for myself every single day), *and* it has also had positive results!

Simply put, wealth witchery is crafting a rich and abundant life with practical wealth manifestation strategies, spells, and rituals, a.k.a. "richuals." It is also connected to a much deeper spiritual practice that transforms your relationship with divine money energies. By learning and implementing these practices, you will be feeling, giving, and receiving money differently than ever before, and with tremendous results!

Richuals are simply rituals that are aligned to abundance. They are a fun way to focus your energy and the energy within your rituals on creating riches every single day. Richuals include wealth practices that can be adapted to your lifestyle, and when used on a consistent basis, they can create a flow of abundance. On this wealth witchery journey, you will learn magical practices that can be integrated into any current daily richuals you already have as a way to amplify your wealth frequency. Once you've read through the practices, it will be totally up to you to determine which feel best for you at any given time. Personally, I like to have a set of richuals that I follow for a month or two before switching them up. Of course, I can include more richuals in my daily practice at any time, and I can replace those that don't feel right anymore.

As you become more and more familiar with these various practices, you will be able to determine your own unique richual practice and routine. For example, if you have five kids, a spouse, and a demanding career, then you might not have a full hour in the morning to spend on your richuals, and you may need to design a time frame that works for you. If you are an entrepreneur and create your own schedule, you may be able to carve out a longer period of time for your practice. The point I want to emphasize is that it is all about what feels most magical for your life and current circumstances.

Of course, part of the work you are doing to create wealth also involves manifesting the type of career, work environment, and hours you want to have in order to create the wealth that supports you best! There is a wonderful domino effect that impacts all areas of your life, including time to do what is most life-giving for you. The more you tap into wealth witchery and money magic, the more you will understand the energies of wealth, which will allow you to manifest at an accelerated rate. The more you practice, the better you get, as with anything in life. Put your whole heart into it, be focused on what you are creating, and show up to do the work. If this sounds a bit overwhelming right now, that's okay. It just means you are at the edge of your comfort zone, and your protective self—the ego mind—does not like it. In chapter 5, I will explain how to take back your power and how to alchemize beliefs that can massively shift your magical practice so resistance does not show up as often. For now, keep reading and know that you are on the path to your success.

The Energy That Is Money

Part of my magical mission is to break the limiting beliefs of the collective consciousness surrounding money. As little kids, many of us were taught that making money is hard work, that we have to suffer for it, or that there is a specific right or wrong way to spend money. The truth is, money is just a form of currency mainly used in this physical reality to get the things that we desire. Like with everything in this world, it is just energy—like you, me, and this book that you are holding. It cannot be a form of evil, have bad intentions, or make people bad because *it is just energy*.

If you were to replace the word *money* with the word *energy*, then some of the beliefs you have about money wouldn't make sense at all! This is an easy way to begin breaking your limiting beliefs. Here are two examples:

1. Money is the root of all evil. → Energy is the root of all evil.
2. There is a limited amount of money. → There is a limited amount of energy.

You can see that in the first example, it doesn't make sense to say that energy is the root of all evil. Therefore, since money is energy, this means that money can't be the root of all evil. There is an unlimited amount of energy in this Universe, so if money is energy, there must be an unlimited amount of it too. There is always enough money and energy to go around because they are infinite. This is a powerful belief I have, and anyone who wants to work with wealth witchery should also adopt it into their belief system because it will automatically put you into an abundance frequency.

As you work with wealth energetics, you will learn that different amounts of money have different vibrational frequencies. For example, manifesting money is like listening to music: A country radio station has a different frequency than a hip-hop station, and you have to be on the right frequency to tune in to what you want. Therefore, if you want to manifest $100, it is a different frequency to attune to than if you were trying to manifest $100,000. As long as you can tune in to the frequency and vibration of the amount of money you desire—and as long as you truly believe you can manifest that amount—then it will come to you. This is what wealth witchery is all about: learning how to expand your consciousness to be able to manifest more wealth into your life. We can only manifest what we think is possible and what our energetic success container can hold. If you have been trying to manifest $100,000 but you haven't even manifested $10,000, then you probably will manifest an amount closer to $10,000 first. The good news is that every time you manifest something toward your goal, more and more opportunities (and money) will expand your energetic container and the consciousness of what you can hold in it, getting you closer and closer to your big money goal. Remember, working with any type of magical craft is a practice. This isn't a get-rich-quick scheme. Rather, in *Wealth Witchery*, you are building a consistent practice that will support you in creating a magical life with the wealth you desire. Manifestation is a skill, and it is a skill you can learn, practice, and master through this book and the continuous implementation of the work and tools within it.

Another hope of mine is that you will explore all the pleasures you desire without holding yourself back. Express who you truly are! Right now, life may seem as if it is determined by the amount of money you have. What you want likely depends on if you can afford it or not. Imagine, for example, that you really want to join a manifestation program or work with a wealth coach because you know that if you join, you will create quantum shifts in your life, but you don't have the money to pay for it right now; you could feel as though you are not able to fully tap into your magic yet because of money. Or let's say you want to buy a pair of sparkly, rainbow-colored platform boots because they resonate strongly with you and would be an expression of your personality, but you do not have the funds to purchase them right now. It would be really disappointing to not be able to have that representation of who you are. I hope these examples illustrate that money could help you show up as your most authentic self and create even more authenticity in your life.

There is a widespread belief that keeps so many people stuck when it comes to manifesting money. That belief is that money cannot buy you happiness, so therefore, money is not important. Wrong! Money *is* important because it is a form of energy we use, as stated earlier. It is the number-one exchange currency to get the things we need in our physical reality. While money can't directly buy anyone happiness, the things that money *can* buy create so much happiness.

When I am happy, I often feel directly aligned to my soul's purpose; it is like a GPS telling me that I am on the right track. If what you desire is truly coming from your heart, then it cannot be wrong—even if it is a pair of Gucci loafers or a Chanel purse. Who is to say that material item is not meant to be yours? I work with a lot of spiritual entrepreneurs, and a major block of theirs is allowing themselves to want and enjoy nice things, because they feel they don't deserve them. It is as if being spiritual means that one is supposed to live a quiet life, giving back to the community and not indulging in any "luxuries." I teach the opposite, and I believe the opposite. Whatever you desire is meant for you. If you want to take a five-day vacation to the Maldives, then do it. There is nothing wrong with filling your own cup and nurturing yourself before you take care of others. You can only show up as your best self if you take care of yourself first. In everyday life and online, I've had people tell me that I shouldn't buy this or invest in that, because it's not worth it. If I had listened to any of those people, I would not be here, writing this book. I would still be working hard, juggling four jobs just to pay my bills. I encourage you to trust your heart, trust your desires, and manifest what you want, even if other people are telling you how silly or selfish they think you are.

In order to call in what you desire, whether it is money or a soulmate, you must already have the vibrational energy of that particular desire within you. You cannot have what you don't already possess within you energetically. To manifest more magic and money, you have to live like you already have it, and *then* it will show up. Remember that we are all energy, so that means we are connected energetically to one another and to all energetic forms. If you feel separated from money and see it as something outside of you that you need to "go get," then you will never have enough, and you will never feel rich.[1] In this book, I will teach you how to show up as the version of yourself who already has what you want and how to make high-level decisions that will help you reach your money goals much faster. This is not "fake it 'til you make it"—this is about you believing and acting as if you have already succeeded. When you show up as the rich witch version of yourself, you will get closer and closer to really being that version of yourself, and that's when the magic happens.

One of my favorite wealth witchery tips is this: If you do not have the physical money or credit to buy something you want, instead of saying "I can't afford this," say, "I choose not to buy this at this time, because I'm putting my money toward something else that is even more amazing." The energy of saying you can't afford something—or, even worse, repeating something like "I am so broke right now"—is the energy of lack. The Universe follows what you focus on. If you focus on how much money you don't have, then the Universe thinks you want to be lacking, so it will send more opportunities to keep you broke. Thoughts and words are very powerful, so make sure you are aware of what you are saying at all times as well as how you are saying it. Even if it is your reality that you don't have the money for something, that doesn't mean

1. Gary M. Douglas, *How to Become Money Workbook* (Access Consciousness Publishing, 2015), Kindle.

this will be your reality forever. You have to choose to focus on embodying abundance in order to call in a different life.

On your wealth witchery journey, it is important to be open to all the ways that money and abundant opportunities may flow into your life. A big mistake many make is thinking money can only come in one way, i.e., the belief that money can only come to us via one person, place, or thing. For the longest time, I thought that money could only come to me from the jobs I was working. For some people, their thinking is that it can only come from their significant other, who is the breadwinner of the family; entrepreneurs may believe money needs to come from one particular program or client. All of this is untrue, because money can come from anywhere and at any time.

One of my clients was making good money via her online program when she came to me for guidance. Her goal was to make $1,000,000 in her business so she could retire and she and her husband could travel the world. After my client shifted her energy and mindset to access a million dollars, she manifested $1,000,000 in her bank account—but it was not from her business. It came in a totally different way, one she never expected at all. My client was able to sell something that her family owned that put the money in her bank account, and her intention was fulfilled. Therefore, when you are doing this work, don't limit your thinking as to how the money or wealth will arrive. Instead, stay open to infinite possibilities.

Your job is to know what you want, align with it, and show up as that version of yourself to manifest it. The job of the Universe is to figure out how to give it to you in the best way possible and make it a reality. While you can definitely put it out there how you'd like something to show up, be open to anything. This is why I always add the phrase "this or something better" to my intentions. By doing so, I am trusting that I will create what I intend in the best way possible for me, including how it comes to me. The only limitations we have are the limits we put on ourselves. Throughout this book, you will learn how to break through your own glass ceiling to manifest your biggest dreams.

Before you move on to the next chapter, there is something I would like you to do. Think of it as an initiation into wealth witchery and being a rich witch. To begin, draw two columns on a piece of paper. In one column, write down all the beautiful, positive thoughts and beliefs you have about money. In the other column, write down all of the limiting beliefs and blockages you have when it comes to money. Even if you think of something you don't consciously believe, write it down. For example, you might want to make more money, but part of you thinks you will have to work harder to make it happen; if so, write that down. Maybe a weird thought bubbles up during this writing practice, something like *Only certain people deserve money*; write that down too. Every thought that pops into your head should be written down, even if you don't think they are true, because those are your subconscious thoughts about money showing up.

The next step is to read the limiting beliefs you wrote down and decide which ones you want to change. Then, write down the belief's opposite, turning negative thoughts into positive affirmations. For example, if your limiting belief is "I believe that I have to work hard for a lot of money," change it to "I am making money so easily every day!" The more you practice creating positive affirmations from your negative thoughts and belief patterns, the easier it will be, and the more awareness you will cultivate and establish as part of your mindset. If you can master this one skill, you will immediately see changes in your life.

TWO
WEALTH WITCHERY TOOLS

Working with magical tools is my secret to manifesting opportunities and accomplishing all my goals. The power of creating the life that you desire comes from your intentions. Everyone has the ability to manifest and to direct magic to call in more abundance, including you! Maybe right now you don't feel as though you are a consistent manifester of your desires; you may be looking to deepen your awareness and practice so that you become one. Or maybe this is the first time you are working with magic, and you are interested in where it can take you. Wherever you are at this point in your journey is perfect.

Working with wealth witchery and other magical practices basically involves using specific tools to bring your thoughts and intentions into physical form. It is also a way of focusing your goals and amplifying what you want to create in your life. Magical tools and/or symbols embody specific energies that help call in your desired results. While you don't actually need physical tools to manifest what you want, I have found that for my clients and myself, it is easier to believe in and strengthen a manifestation when we are using something tangible, something we can see and hold. It is a lot of fun to activate spells and rituals with magical tools.

In this chapter, you will learn about some of the tools I typically work with to enhance my magic and manifestation spells. You may choose to combine some of the tools or just use them one at a time—it is up to you. Begin to use your magical intuition!

Petition Paper

Many witches and magical practitioners like to write the intentions for their spells or rituals on special paper. This particular tool is typically called a *petition paper*. As implied in the name, you are petitioning a source (the Universe, or whomever you are connecting with) to help you manifest your goals. There are no specific rules you have to follow in regard to the kind of paper it needs to be or its size. Simply having a dedicated type of paper that you only use when you are doing magic can help boost your practice and quickly manifest your desires.

Personally, I like to cut my petition papers into squares and anoint them with various abundance oils, especially for spells focused on increasing my wealth. You can also cut them into stars, hearts, or another shape that resonates with you to enhance your magic. If you don't feel like cutting paper, you can buy some origami paper and use it as premade petition paper. Additionally, I like to use gold petition paper for the spells and richuals in this book because the color gold signifies wealth and prosperity.

Candles

Candles are very popular tools used by magical practitioners. Depending on your intention, you can customize the shape, size, and color of the candle, which may help you achieve your goals more quickly. It is very easy to work with candles in your wealth witchery practice. Candle magic activates the element of fire, which represents passion, illumination, and transformation. You can light one candle or combine multiple candles for even more magic.

The easiest way to understand how to work with candles is to start with color magic. Simply put, the energy of each color has a different meaning or significance; therefore, you may want to choose a colored candle that corresponds with what you most want to manifest. This is a technique that you can use with crystals also, which will be explained later on in this chapter.

Here are some candle colors and their corresponding descriptions related to manifesting money and abundance.

White	Connected to spirituality, cleansing, and clearing, and can be used to represent any color if you don't have a particular color of candle
Black	Protection and repelling negative energy
Brown	Grounding and embodiment
Orange	Opens the roads for success and instant gratification
Yellow	Success, happiness, and fame
Green	Prosperity, money, healing, and abundance
Gold	Money, abundance, and wealth; this is the color I like to use for money spells
Red	Magnetic attraction and passion
Pink	Unconditional love and harmony
Purple	Intuition, psychic awareness, and wisdom

Selecting the type of candle (or candles) you use will depend on how long your spell or richual is going to last. If you don't have much time to sit around and wait for the candle to burn down completely, you can use a birthday candle, which burns for around five to fifteen minutes. Tea lights are also easy and fast candles to work with. The candles that I normally use for my spells are chime spell candles, which you can get online or at a metaphysical store; chime candles burn for one to two hours. For your altar and for extended magical work, you can use large pillar or votive candles. Beeswax candles are one of the best types of candles to work with when doing spells because they are natural and conduct magic very well. However, feel free to choose the type of wax and candle that resonates with you.

Another pro tip when working with candles associated with manifestation and magic is to inscribe your intention or some power words into the candle. I was taught to write my intention in an upward direction, from base to wick, when calling in something desired. If, however, the intention is to clear out and/or release something, the intention can be written in a downward direction, from the wick to the base. You can use the same method and guidelines when applying anointing oil to your candles.

Lots of people use candleholders for their spells and richuals, but you can also use a plate or other firesafe object to hold your candle. A helpful tip when using a plate or free-standing object is to melt the bottom of your candle with fire before lighting the wick. Then, stick the melted bottom of the candle onto a plate or other object. The wax will harden, and the candle should be secure. You can then light the wick.

When you are working with candles, always make sure that you are keeping an eye on your candle the entire time it is burning in order to maintain safety. I've had candles fly off the plate and onto my carpet as well as other issues that needed my immediate attention, so it's very important to be careful when using candles.

If you'd like to take your candle magic to the next level, you can also do an assessment of the wax after the candle has burnt down. Simply take a look at what shapes or symbols you see in the melted wax. Know that there is no right or wrong way to do this. What is important is what you see and how you interpret it. This is so fascinating to do! I've seen dinosaurs and peacocks in my wax and many, many other interesting symbols, all of which meant something to me based on the specific spell I was doing. The images that catch your eye can provide insights, guidance, and even the next steps for you to take after activating that particular spell. Reading images in candle wax may take some practice, but the more you work to discovering the symbols and tap into your own magical guidance, the easier it will be.

Remember, there is no right or wrong way to read the wax or do candle magic, so just trust that your way is the perfect, divine way for you. The most powerful thing to do when working with candle magic is to allow yourself a spark of curiosity. Have fun with it!

The Chakras

Just like the liver and kidneys are organs that help the physical body function, chakras are the energy organs for our energetic bodies. The word *chakra* comes from the Sanskrit word *cakra*, meaning "wheel," and they are often described as a spinning vortex or wheel of energy.[2] I believe that there are different points in the body where energy flows and converges. These energy centers are an important part of your wealth witchery journey because they will help you

---

2. *Merriam-Webster Dictionary*, "chakra," accessed May 10, 2024, https://www.merriam-webster.com/dictionary/chakra.

stay grounded and reach the next level of abundance. Chakras regulate and are associated with different aspects of physical, emotional, mental, and spiritual well-being.

There are many chakras in our bodies, but the practices in this book will work with the seven main chakras along the central channel of the body, starting from the base of the spine and extending to the crown of the head. Our goal for chakra magic is to balance and align these energy centers. When a chakra is balanced, energy flows freely through it, creating more health, abundance, and magic in your life. When a chakra is blocked, it can lead to physical and emotional challenges.

Each of the seven chakras has a different color associated with it; this visual can help you focus your attention and intention on balancing and healing these energy centers.

Here are the seven major chakras and how you can work with them on your wealth witchery journey.

Root Chakra

Positioned at the base of the spine, the root chakra represents stability, security, and the connection to the material world. It is where we should root all manifestations and beliefs. To work with the root chakra for financial abundance, focus on making your new goals feel safe for you. Often, if you are repelling your manifestations, it is because the ego is trying to protect you. It does not know if this new opportunity will hurt you, so to be safe, the ego creates doubts and beliefs to keep you stuck where you are. Affirmations like "I am financially secure" can be powerful.

The color of the root chakra is red.

Chakra figure

Sacral Chakra

The sacral chakra governs creativity, passion, divine femininity, and abundance. This is the energy center where you can ignite your money manifestations. When you are setting intentions or creating a dream board for your goals, this is the chakra that is being activated. When your sacral chakra is balanced, creative ideas flow through you and activate powerful manifestation energies.

The sacral chakra is located right below your belly button, and the color of this chakra is orange.

Solar Plexus Chakra

This is the energetic center for personal power, motivation, action, self-esteem, and confidence. The solar plexus chakra builds on the creative ideas and energies of the sacral chakra, taking action to make these ideas a reality. Having an open and clear solar plexus chakra will help you feel motivated to accomplish your goals.

The solar plexus chakra is located near your stomach and is associated with the color yellow.

Heart Chakra

The heart chakra represents love, gratitude, and compassion. It is the energy center for attracting what you desire. This is also the chakra that can hold the expansion that you are creating. Working on your heart chakra will allow you to hold more money, opportunity, and success. Being in love, kindness, and gratitude are all powerful practices in balancing the heart chakra.

The color of this chakra is green or, for some people, pink.

Throat Chakra

Located at your throat, this energy center focuses on clear communication and speaking your truth. When your throat chakra is open and balanced, you will be able to articulate your money intentions clearly and powerfully. Your words are your wand—what you speak creates your reality. Singing and chanting are also powerful ways to work with your throat chakra to manifest more abundance.

The color of this chakra is blue.

Third Eye Chakra

The third eye chakra is located in the middle of your forehead, between your eyebrows. I like to visualize this as an eye. When my third eye chakra is balanced, it is violet and wide open with beautiful eyelashes. When it is unbalanced or blocked, I imagine my third eye closed and crusted over. The third eye chakra enhances intuition and insight and enables you to make informed choices. It is also where you can send out your manifestations—your vision—to the Universe. Having a balanced third eye chakra will allow you to trust your inner wisdom when making decisions.

The third eye chakra is usually depicted in visualizations as an indigo energy center.

Crown Chakra

The crown chakra resides right above your head, and it connects you to higher spiritual realms and universal abundance, providing a sense of purpose and alignment with your highest-level goals. Meditation and mindfulness can help you connect to your crown chakra and the universal flow of abundance to manifest more prosperity. When the reason you want to manifest more money is aligned with your morals and your spiritual values (whatever and whomever you believe in), then you will find that money easily flows to you.

The crown chakra can be a white light or, as I prefer to imagine, a thousand-petal rainbow lotus.

Anointing Oils

You might be familiar with essential oils, which are essences extracted from a plant in concentrated form.[3] Anointing oils, also known as spiritual oils, take the use of essential oils a step further. Anointing oils incorporate essential oils but are already mixed with carrier oils to dilute them. They are created through ceremonies and rituals in which a unique blend has been prayed over or blessed. You can make your own anointing oils or purchase them from magical practitioners you trust; my favorite place to shop for anointing oils is via Madame Pamita (www.parlourofwonders.com).

What I love about using anointing oils is they indicate exactly what the energy of the oil is and what it is best used for, so when purchasing an anointing oil, you do not have to look up its uses or try to guess what type of magical spell to incorporate it into. Once purchased, anointing oils can be enhanced with herbs, crystals, or even pieces of fake dollar bills for use as a money oil.

You can use anointing oils to activate the energy of your intention by rubbing the oil on your body or on the items you use as part of your magical process. Anointing oil can also amplify the energy of a candle you are using in your spell or richual; simply rub some anointing oil on the candle before lighting the wick.

If you don't know where to start, here are some potent anointing oils I use in my wealth witchery practice.

---

3. Working with essential oils is very magical, but it is also important to use them carefully, since they are very powerful and very potent. Before applying them on the skin, a pure essential oil must be blended with a carrier oil (like almond, jojoba, or coconut oil) to dilute the essential oil.

Anointing Oil	Purpose
Instant Gratification	Brings immediate outcomes and collapses time to achieve your goals
Open Roads	Clears the obstacles that are blocking you from your success
Good Luck	Brings in luck and fortune in your particular situation and helps things go your way
Bountiful Blessings	Calls in miracles and blessings to manifest your best life
Abundant Prosperity	Activates abundant financial opportunities that will flow into your life
Money Magnet	Attracts money and increases funds in your bank account easily
Grand Success	Helps you achieve your goals and guarantees success with ease and grace
Magnetic Attraction	Acts like a magnet to draw abundance and all of your desires to you
Joie De Vivre	Brings in the potent energies of happiness and joy for prosperity
Fame and Fortune	Draws attention to you so that you can be recognized for your abilities, skills, or magic

Herbs

Natural elements like herbs are filled with powerful magic and energy, and working with them is an ancient practice passed down in many cultures. Plants are alive with specific frequencies that we seek for spells and richuals. I believe that there are spirits residing in plants, and that we can honor and work with them to achieve our goals.

There are a few ways that you can gather herbs. One way is to start an herb garden and grow them yourself. They are usually pretty easy to grow. Of course, you can also just buy them at the store! You don't need to go to a metaphysical store, as most of the plants in this section should be available to purchase at any supermarket. If you are growing and cutting the plants yourself, however, please do so with respect for the plant. Before cutting off a piece of the plant, speak to the plant and share what you are going to be doing with the herb. Afterward, thank the plant. This will ensure the plant will continue to help and provide for you!

When you are adding herbs to your magical work, you will notice that certain ones seem to work better for you than others. Eventually, you will intuitively know which herbs you prefer for various types of richuals. To help you keep track of this and other important feedback you obtain during spell work, it helps to write down your process, the ingredients used, and other details of your magical experiments and experiences in a magical grimoire, otherwise known as a Book of Shadows. Your Book of Shadows could be a binder or a notebook. As you track the results of your magic, you will begin to notice which herbs call in money the fastest as well as other important details. By doing this, you will also be able to cultivate a custom list of the ingredients you like most, as well as the ingredients that have the best results.

I have included a list of herbs in this section. These are the magical herbs I like to use in my prosperity spells. Most of these you probably already have in your kitchen cabinet or spice rack!

Herb	Magical Correspondences
Alfalfa	Money, prosperity, and luck
Allspice	Luck and money
Basil	Wealth, good fortune, and peace
Cinnamon	Prosperity, success, and luck
Cloves	Abundance, money, and protection
Ginger	Speeds up manifestation and brings in money
Lavender	Happiness and protection; increases potency of spell
Rose	Beauty, love, and healing
Rosemary	Cleansing and clearing
Mint	Prosperity, money, and protection
Pumpkin spice	This spice contains many of the money herbs shared here
Sunflower	Success, victory, and happiness

Tarot

Using tarot as an element to power up manifestations is a must. Tarot is a deck of seventy-eight cards. Each card has various meanings and includes multiple symbols in the artwork. The unique system of tarot includes twenty-two major arcana cards, forty minor arcana cards, and sixteen court cards. The major arcana cards represent big events in our lives such as giving birth, getting married, traveling overseas, or new relationships and careers. The minor arcana cards are divided into four suits that include the creative, fiery energy of the Wands; the emotional, watery energy of the Cups; the intelligent, airy energy of the Swords; and the abundant, earthly energy of the Pentacles. Each suit is composed of ten cards, ace through ten, and these cards often represent everyday life experiences. The court cards represent the growth or expansion of one's journey from the experience of being a Page, or a student, learning a new way of doing things, to the Knight, who is the action taker, to the Queen, who has obtained mastery in a specific area, to the King, who has evolved to the role of leader. This popular tool is used for many purposes, including divination readings, predicting the future, self-development, and so much more. Tarot cards can even be included in spells and richuals!

You don't need to be a master of tarot or even a tarot reader to include tarot in your magic. However, I strongly suggest that you get somewhat familiar with the specific card(s) you want to use prior to incorporating them in a spell. After you have chosen your card(s), the first thing I suggest doing is writing down what meanings, clues, and/or feelings the artwork inspires. Next, look up what that particular card means in the guidebook provided with the deck. With these new insights, determine if this card is in fact one you want to use in your spell. If you are an advanced magical practitioner, you can also tap into the energy of the cards and ask questions. A good question to ask may be if the card wants to work with you to help you reach your goals. If you are a novice reader, you can still ask the deck questions by pulling a card. If you need help determining the answer, use the guidebook that is provided with the deck.

In addition to familiarizing yourself with the deck prior to use, rely on your intuition when choosing which card or cards to use for a particular magical process. Carefully look through the cards to see what imagery stands out to you. Do any of the cards seem to be calling out to you? They may want to work with you!

If you are curious about tarot or interested in adding this magical tool to your practice, here is a cheat sheet for using tarot in wealth witchery. These are the cards I use in my manifestation magic because they are all, in some capacity, tied to the magic of abundance. If a card that resonates with you is not on this list, that doesn't mean it is not the right one to work with or that it won't help you; follow your magical guidance and select what feels right for you.

Tarot Card	Magical Correspondences
The Sun	Victory and success
Wheel of Fortune	Good luck and fortune
The Star	Hope and success
The World	Completion and celebration
The Empress	Luxury and wealth
The Emperor	Leadership and CEO magic
Ace of Pentacles	New opportunities and plenty of material resources
Three of Pentacles	Formation of a powerful team
Six of Pentacles	Donations and gifts of money
Eight of Pentacles	Manifestation of money and material resources
Nine of Pentacles	Wealth and success
Ten of Pentacles	Legacy and prosperity
Queen of Pentacles	An increase of money and abundance

Tarot Card	Magical Correspondences
King of Pentacles	Leadership; the ultimate money-making card
Ace of Cups	Abundance and inspiration
Two of Cups	Partnership and collaboration
Nine of Cups	Wishes coming true
Ten of Cups	Happiness and fulfillment

Crystals

One of the very first magical tools I used in my spells and richuals were crystals. The frequency held in each crystal can naturally connect with your energetic field to amplify the magic you want to work with. Using crystals to shift your energy and to manifest prosperity can be as easy as putting one on your altar, keeping one in your wallet, or meditating with them. Each crystal will tell you how it wants to work with you; you may receive a thought or a feeling as to where your crystal wants to go or what it wants to do. Though at first you may wonder if these are your own thoughts, trust that these messages are really the crystal communicating with you.

Crystals are very powerful tools you can add to any magical practice, ritual, or spell. Here are the main prosperity crystals I work with to magnify the energy of abundance.

Citrine

There are two different kinds of citrine. One is heat treated, and the other is its natural and pure form. Most people don't know that darker orange and yellow citrine, which both come in clusters, are heat-treated amethyst or smoky quartz. Real citrine is only sold as a tower or point and is a clear yellow color.

I only work with real citrine in my rituals and spells, but at times I do enjoy having the energies of heat-treated citrine around me. The energies of real citrine and heat-treated citrine are going to feel different for everyone. Personally, I've found that real citrine feels like I'm linked up to the Ritz-Carlton and it's sending me generational wealth magic, whereas heat-treated citrine is more of a quick money boost for me. It is up to you which kind of citrine you'd like to work with.

Citrine is one of the most powerful abundance stones I have worked with, and the best thing about this crystal is that you don't need to recharge it. Like the sun, citrine is always in a bright, happy mood. Citrine also holds the energy of motivation and joy. Keep a citrine tower on your desk or near where you make money for continuous and increased abundance.

Pyrite

Pyrite is also known as "fool's gold," as it only contains a tiny percentage of gold even though the entire crystal is a metallic, brassy color. The energy of pyrite can help spark new ideas, increase confidence, encourage wealth, and attract success. I like to keep my pyrite crystals on my altar, cultivating a powerful, rich space for my money magic.

Green Aventurine

Green aventurine is an affordable and common stone. This abundance crystal works with the heart chakra to amplify your money magnetism. It can also bring in new opportunities, activate courage, and promote happiness. The best way to work with green aventurine is to keep small, tumbled stones in your pocket or even your bra, or you can wear it as jewelry. Keeping the stone close to you will actively attract prosperity into your life.

Tiger's Eye

Tiger's eye is a beautiful crystal that is striped with black, brown, and/or gold. When you move this crystal around, the luster sparkles and looks like a tiger's eye. This crystal is also known as the "gambler's stone," bringing good luck and fortune to the owner. Tiger's eye is a powerful stone for self-confidence, protection, clarity, and new possibilities. My favorite way of working with tiger's eye is to hold the crystal in my hand when I gamble.

Clear Quartz

This crystal is also known as the master healing stone, and it greatly amplifies your intentions or the energies of any other crystals in your spells. You can put a clear quartz tower in the center of a crystal grid to maximize its energy, or you can set it on any part of your body that needs healing. If you don't have the crystal that you need, you can use clear quartz as a substitute to manifest the other crystal's energy. Clear quartz can also promote protection when you are driving or traveling.

You might come across other crystals that are ideal for your manifestation that were not in this section. If you feel called to a certain crystal, then use it! It really is that simple. Play with the crystals that bring you the most joy and feel right for your practice.

Just having a crystal around you may bring good vibes and prosperity. However, it is always best to work with crystal magic based on intention. Before working with a crystal, give it a good cleanse by leaving it outside under the light of the full moon or by giving it a smoke cleanse with purifying herbs. Then, hold the crystal to your heart and tell it what your intentions are and how you want it to work with you. Imagine yourself connecting to the energy of the crystal, and either keep the crystal with you at all times or set it someplace important, like your altar or next to your bed.

When you are done working with a crystal, you can cleanse it and recharge it the same way as before. When working with crystals, remember they are just as alive as you are, and because of that, there is always ongoing communication between you both. Trust your intuition and your feelings about how to work with each crystal. If you want to dive deeper into your crystal magic practice, you can find more helpful information in my book *Enchanted Crystal Magic: Spells, Grids & Potions to Manifest Your Desires.*

Days of the Week

Each day of the week is connected to a certain planet and a certain energy, and all are associated with a specific frequency that can benefit your wealth witchery practice. By choosing the day of the week that corresponds with what you want to manifest, you can supercharge your magic. Take a look at what each day represents, and incorporate this information in your spells and richuals.

Sunday Magic

Sundays are super easy to remember because the ruling planet is in the name: the sun. The energies related to this day are happiness, success, prosperity, new opportunities, growth, and money.

Monday Magic

Many people start their work week on Monday, and they may dread this day of the week. But the magic of Mondays might make all who dread it rethink how this day should be viewed. Monday is actually connected to the moon. If you have a spell that is related to the moon, you can always cast it on this day, regardless of the current lunar phase. The energies for this day are related to emotions, dreams, mysteries, intuition, psychic awareness, and spirituality.

Tuesday Magic

Tuesdays are powerful days, as they are ruled by the masculine energy of Mars. If you need some courage to express your passion and truth, today is the day to share what's on your mind. The energies connected to this day are passion, success, justice, confidence, and protection. This is a great day for spells related to work, business, or legal issues.

Wednesday Magic

Wednesday is the day of communication, ruled by the planet Mercury. This is the most magical day for speaking, sharing your thoughts, writing, and anything that has to do with intellect. The energies represented on this day are tied to technology, spiritual growth, communication, traveling, divination, intuition, and clarity.

Thursday Magic

One of my favorite days for money magic is Thursday, which is the day connected to the planet Jupiter. Jupiter is connected to the energy of success and prosperity. For this reason, most of my spells for abundance are done on this day. The energies represented by

Thursdays are wealth, material success, luck, health, ambition, and leadership.

Friday Magic

Another great day for manifestation is Friday, the day ruled by the planet Venus. The energy of Venus is all about magnetism and attraction, as well as the magic of inviting in new opportunities, new projects, and new relationships. The energy of this day is related to relationships, love, emotion, the divine feminine, passion, attraction, and beauty.

Saturday Magic

This is another day with a planetary correspondence that is easy to remember, as the word *Saturday* has part of the word *Saturn* in it! The planet Saturn rules over maturity, responsibility, and discipline. The energies of this day are related to protection, personal and spiritual development, learning, transformation, releasing, and meditation.

Lunar Cycle Magic

A popular magical tool to use with manifesting is the lunar cycle. The moon travels through eight phases, and within each of these phases, it holds a different energy. The energy and magnetism of the moon is so powerful that it even impacts the tides of Earth's oceans. Harnessing the potent energies of the moon will magnify your manifestation.

Working with moon magic is a journey through each of the phases, as each stage correlates to and empowers your manifestations. To that end, one of the most effective ways to integrate moon magic is to focus on one intention for an entire lunar cycle, with each cycle starting at the new moon and moving through the next seven phases with the same intention or goal. Each particular phase will infuse your intention with its energy and will also guide the active steps you are taking as you bring your intention into physical reality.

In this section, I'll share a little bit about the eight phases of the moon and how you can start to incorporate them in your wealth witchery practice.

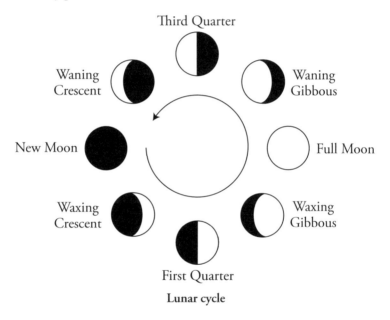

Lunar cycle

New Moon Magic

The new moon is the first phase of the lunar cycle. It is also known as the dark moon because the illuminated side of the moon is facing away from Earth, making it hard to see in the night sky. When the moon is "new," the energy during this time represents new beginnings. It is the perfect time to set new intentions and manifest new opportunities. In my wealth witchery practice, I do a new moon candle spell every month.

Waxing Crescent Moon Magic

During the waxing crescent moon phase, the moon grows in its illumination, and so too can your manifestation. During this time, be very clear about what you want and how you want to show up in your life. Imagine the highest version of yourself, the version that most reflects how you want to express yourself, and focus on the details of this future self. Write out what you most want to be and do in your life, and dream big. Based on this best version of yourself, craft a plan that is aligned with your goal. Imagine that you have already achieved your goal; what would the path to getting there look like? Then, write down the steps to reach your goal as if you have already manifested it.

First Quarter Moon Magic

During this phase, it is time to bring everything you visualized in your waxing crescent action plan into physical reality, meaning it is time to take some action! Start by taking the first few steps toward achieving your goal.

Waxing Gibbous Moon Magic

During the waxing gibbous moon, it is time for reflection and refinement. The momentum of your manifestation is building, as is the magic of the moon. If you are feeling stuck on any of the steps in your action plan, or if you are not seeing things starting to manifest the way you would like, perhaps you need to change things up or move things around to achieve your goal. Take another look at your plan and see if you need to shift any of your next steps. Either way, keep pushing through.

Full Moon Magic

By the time this phase of the moon appears, you should have seen some movement toward your goal. Your intention may have already manifested! If your intention has not manifested yet, don't give up. Maybe your manifestation process is missing something and just needs to be adjusted, or maybe it will show up during the next lunar cycle. Either way, this is a beautiful time of healing and of releasing anything that does not currently support you on your path.

Remember, you can only manifest what your consciousness can hold at any given time. Every time you manifest even a part of what you want (for example, if you are in the process of manifesting $10,000 and you have only received $2,000), you are expanding your energetic container even more, and as it expands further, you will be able to fully call in the abundance you desire.

Waning Gibbous Moon Magic

The most powerful fuel for manifestation is gratitude. During the waning gibbous moon, the focus is on being thankful for all of the things you already have. However, it's not only about saying or writing what you are thankful for. In order for gratitude magic to contribute to the fulfillment of your intentions, you have to feel it. This means you have to allow yourself to feel deep gratitude throughout your being. This is an important practice throughout all the lunar phases, but it is especially potent during this time.

Third Quarter Moon Magic

The third quarter moon is the phase for releasing and letting go of stagnant energy. You can also apply this to the physical realm by cleaning out material things that are taking up space in your home or office. If you have habits that you want to change, this is the time to release them and shift into new ways of doing things. Clear out what is no longer serving you to make space for the things you want.

Waning Crescent Moon Magic

The waning crescent moon phase is all about surrender. During this magical phase, you are called to relax and rest. The new moon is about to arrive again, and this time is best used to reset so that you are ready for the next round of manifestation. It is also a good time to end projects or relationships that are no longer supporting you.

While creating your most abundant life and working with wealth witchery doesn't require the use of magical tools, there are many to choose from that can enhance your magical experience. Remember to use magical tools that resonate for you at any given time. If none of these tools are resonating, then don't use any at all! But, if you are like me and love to add candles, crystals, and oils to your craft, then do so. Utilize whatever you feel will create the most magical space for your intentions to manifest. Most of all, always remember that magic is already within you, and it gets activated when you are in alignment with your bliss. As long as you feel good about what you are doing and how you are doing it, then you can manifest anything you desire.

THREE
ABUNDANCE ALTARS

Manifestation, which is attracting what you most desire, has two main components you will always be working with: One is connected to the material world and the other is connected to the energetic, magical world. First, you must shift and align your energetic self to your desires through devotional practices like rituals, ceremonies, and spells. This will guide you to take action in the material world as you shift your physical reality to match those desires. Working with an abundance altar taps into both of these aspects of manifestation and can help you stay in the magical flow of receptivity to manifestation—in this case, to more and more wealth.

Not everyone can manifest through a money mindset alone; many people benefit from something more. Altars can be that something more. An abundance altar is an important element of wealth witchery. It is a sacred space dedicated to crafting your wealth and the intuitive process. When you create an altar, you are creating a vortex of energy that is always there to support you and guide you in the manifestation of your goals. Your altar can reconnect you to your soul's desires and the vibrational frequency of the future you are creating. Think of establishing and using an abundance altar as a foolproof way to manifest prosperity.

An abundance altar, like all altars, is spiritually charged with your magic and the energies of the cosmos to propel you to manifest your intentions. Just like the use of magical tools, there is no right or wrong way to use an abundance altar. In this chapter, I will share simple steps, techniques, and tools that you may choose to use to create your own altar, but ultimately, it is up to you to pick and choose how you want to build your abundance altar. Trust your intuition.

Setting Up Your Abundance Altar

When creating an abundance altar, make choices that resonate with you. What your altar looks like is not as important as your connection to it.

Choosing a Space for Your Abundance Altar

When you read the word *altar*, do you picture a huge temple with big statues? I used to think of an altar as something huge and elaborate because of all the Buddhist temples I went to when I was younger. What I have discovered is that an altar can be as big and fancy or as minimal and cozy as you want. You can also have an altar anywhere in your house. Simply find a space that feels private yet accessible so you will make it a main focus of your abundance practice. You can put your altar on a table, shelf, cabinet, or even on a windowsill if you don't have a lot of room. The size of your altar does not matter—it's the magic that lies within it, and as a part of it, that makes all the difference. Make sure that your altar will be disturbed as little as possible; I have had clients create altars in closets or drawers because they have kids or cats that knock everything over.

You may want to have a few different altars around your home. I currently have three money and abundance altars scattered throughout my office and home. Every time I walk by and glance at these altars, I am reminded to tap into the frequency of my rich witch future self, and doing so amplifies my abundance even more. If you travel a great deal, you may want to add a traveling altar. I will share more specific information about travel altars later in this chapter.

Brainstorming Your Abundance Altar

There are some questions you may want to ask yourself before constructing an altar. The first question is, what is your purpose in creating this specific altar? For many people, when an altar is related to abundance, it is to manifest a certain amount of money. If that is true for you, establish your intention for your altar. Ask yourself why you want this money and what you want to use it for. For example, is it to buy a new home or take your dream vacation? Be very specific about your "why." Perhaps you are making an altar dedicated to overall abundance in your life. In this case, you could detail what your life would look like if you were abundant. What would you be doing for work if you were wealthy? What would your health be like? How would your relationships be affected? Go as in-depth as you want. Above all, have fun exploring the reason for creating your abundance altar. Once you have set an intentional focus for your abundance altar, make sure you have your intention written on your altar somewhere visible.

Next, ask yourself if you want your altar to invoke any deities or energies. There are many guides, deities, and high-vibe energies that can help you reach your goals. If you choose to work with a god, goddess, celestial being, cosmic energy, ancestor, angel, unicorn, or any other guide, you can dedicate your abundance altar to them. If you typically work with your own guides, they can also assist with your altar as long as you ask for their help. Working with a magical being is totally optional—you do not need to dedicate your altar to anyone if you don't want to.

If invoking a new energetic being resonates with you, do some research to discover which deities or energies like to work with abundance and wealth. When you have chosen one magical being, connect with them to see if they actually want to work with you at this time. To do this, simply close your eyes and picture the magical being you'd like to invoke in your mind's eye. Then, ask if they want to work with you. If you feel, hear, or see the answer "No," then thank them graciously and move on to another magical being. If you feel, hear, or see "Yes," then congratulations, you now have a magical guide who is going to powerfully support you on your journey! I recommend researching what your guide's symbols are (if they have any), what they like, and different ways they can be honored; you can incorporate all of that in your practice if you wish.

As an example, one of my favorite deities to work with in my wealth witchery practice is Lakshmi. She is the Hindu goddess of abundance and is always ready to work with me. I know Lakshmi loves roses and seashells, so I sprinkle them across my altar. During my work with her, I give her offerings of food and drinks, and I recite or sing her powerful mantra 108 times daily for abundance. The first time I worked with her, I was able to manifest a revenue of $10,000 per month for my business!

No matter which magical being shows up for you at any given time, know they will be the perfect abundance guide to work with for whatever you are focused on manifesting. If a guide you really wanted to work with tells you "No," don't be discouraged. You might not be ready for their teachings, or they may know that another guide is a better fit. You can always circle back to a guide who told you "No" at a later date.

When creating an altar, you should follow your heart every step of the way, as you must believe your altar is bringing you what you most desire and is in alignment with your best, truest self. Always be intentional regarding an altar's purpose, the energy you are activating through it, and what it will do for you. For example, maybe your intention is that every time you work at your altar, unexpected money comes into your life. Hence, when you pass by your altar, you will feel uplifted and expansive.

Activating Your Abundance Altar

Once you have selected the perfect magical tools for your abundance altar, cleanse the space where you will be setting it up. You can cleanse it by burning herbs like rosemary and lavender or using high-vibrational sprays. Next, start setting up your altar with magical tools. Let your heart guide you. If you want to put something on the edge of your altar, do it; if you want to make everything symmetrical, do that. Tap into your creative side and let go of trying to make everything perfect.

After setting up your altar, you can activate it by lighting a candle and stating your intention for this space. I like to call in my guides and/or the Universe to assist me in my goals, so I may say something like, "Creator of all that is, cosmos, celestial guides, angels, and unicorns, I illuminate this candle to call upon you to bless and activate this sacred space. Guide me with clarity to [insert goal]. Thank you, thank you, thank you, and so it is." Now you are ready for all the magic!

Establishing a Practice

If you have created an altar before, you may already have a consistent devotional practice you use to activate and honor your altars. If you don't currently have a devotional practice, or if you would like to modify or change the one you have, then you can integrate some of the ideas in this chapter.

If you are a beginner when it comes to altar work, I suggest developing a daily practice associated with your altar because that is a great way to start building up magical energy. If you are a more experienced altar practitioner, then craft your devotional time with your altar however you feel guided.

Most importantly, once you activate an altar, you should use it and tend to it on a regular basis.

Working at Your Abundance Altar

In this section, I have included some ideas of things you could do at your abundance altar. Try them out and see which practices resonate with you. You may combine one, two, or all of them, or you may want to switch it up depending on how you feel on any given day.

Candle Magic

Create a simple activation or prayer to honor your altar space, then light a candle. You may also use the candle as an intention candle and ask for what you desire. I do this daily. If you are working with a specific deity or energy, you can invoke them when lighting the candle.

Meditation

It is very powerful to sit in the energy of your abundance altar and meditate. Some people clear their mind when they meditate. Personally, my favorite thing to do when I meditate is find inspiration in the creative thoughts that flow to me after my mind has been cleared of any doubts or fears. Instead of trying to push all thoughts away, try to be open to fun, expansive thoughts that can inspire you as you release those that are not serving you. When you are centered and grounded in your breath and body and you feel peaceful, let your mind wander and start exploring. Daydream and see what possibilities, thoughts, and ideas are ready to appear. I usually get the idea for my next book, deck, or program during these mediations. Allow yourself to relax and enjoy the inspired thoughts that come.

Journaling

Doing journal work in front of your altar can instantly put you into the magical state you need to be in to channel the highest version of yourself and receive the downloads required for your daily inspired actions. I share a system of journaling that is related to abundance as well as other helpful tips in chapter 8 of this book.

Chanting Mantras

Chanting mantras in your sacred space creates even more positive, high-vibe energy around your intentions. There are many abundance mantras you can chant, including simple one-word chants such as "Ah" or "Om." As I shared previously, when I work with Lakshmi, I chant her abundance mantra 108 times a day. Why 108? That's the number of vital points of the life force, known as *marma points*; there are 107 in the body and one in the head, according to Ayurveda. These are points in the physical body that are connected to your higher self. Altars and mantras support us in connecting the spiritual self and the physical self; they bring both together to manifest our desires.

Search for a mantra that resonates with you in regard to your intention, or make up your own. One of my favorite mantras I have worked with is "Money flows easily to me." It can be that simple, but it should be something that really resonates with you. Once you have your mantra, chant it from your belly and out through your third eye chakra, which sits in the middle of your forehead. My voice alchemy teacher says to imagine you've grown a unicorn horn and your mantra is vibrating out of it.

Like everything else, always chant your mantras with intention and confidence. When you chant, you are not just saying words and being loosey-goosey with them—that will never work. Instead, infuse the energy of your intention into every cell of the body. Then, the energetic field receives it and believes it is true.

Cartomancy

Cartomancy is one of the easiest ways to connect to your intuition and divination. Divination is the act of receiving messages from your soul and the Universe, and cartomancy is the reading of cards. You may use tarot cards or oracle cards to assist you in this practice. Whichever deck calls out to you at any given time is the one you are meant to work with. If you have more than one deck, you can also designate one for your altar specifically for this work.

The most effective and simple way to incorporate cartomancy into your altar work is to shuffle the cards, ask one question related to what you are wanting to manifest, and pull one card. Make sure that your question is an empowering one, perhaps something like, "What can I change or take action on today to help me reach my goal easily and quickly?" Another idea is to simply pull a card for the energy and message of the day.

I like to dive into the art and symbolism of the card first to see what messages I intuitively receive. Next, I pick up the guidebook that accompanies the deck to see if anything else related to this card stands out to me. Finally, I put it all together for a powerful message that guides me and my journey.

I recommend that you write down all the thoughts that came up for you during a reading, maybe even before doing any of the other steps. With all of these steps, trust that whatever comes up is your message, even if it sounds like you are talking to yourself.

Visualization

Visualization is one of the most powerful modalities to utilize as a tool for the manifestation of your desires. I incorporate visualization every single day. When I do this, I always see what I want as if it has already happened. I believe this is how I have been able to manifest so much money and so many opportunities as quickly as I have. When you imagine and visualize your goals as if they have already happened, your brain does not know if that visualization is fake or if it is real. If you can think your future into reality consistently, your brain and your energetic body will draw in the opportunities that will get you to that place.

A potent technique to use along with visualization is a manifestation board. A manifestation board is basically a vision board on which you put all of your goals in the form of pictures, words, or even drawings that represent what you desire. In chapter 6, you will discover how to create a Prosperity Dream Board, which can support you in reaching your goals. Remember, what you focus on the most is what comes into your life. Therefore, if you keep seeing visual representations of your goal, then your subconscious mind will always be focusing on it, even if you don't consciously think of it. Creating a manifestation board is a physical action you can take to bring your intentions and thoughts into the material world. When you add a manifestation board to your altar, it is being charged and powered up by all the positive vibes that surround it every day through your energy and focus. It also keeps the space super focused on your dreams.

Crystal Magic

Crystal magic is one of my favorite ways to work with energy! Definitely have crystals on and around your abundance altar, if at all possible. The energy of the crystals helps amplify the energy of the space.

You can program a crystal with your intention at your altar. This is a super simple magical practice that creates phenomenal results. With your intention in mind, choose a crystal that you are drawn to, perhaps one that is energetically connected to your goals so you can achieve them faster. Next, sit in your sacred space in front of your altar and hold the crystal to your heart. Close your eyes and command your intention into your crystal. Always speak as if your intention has already come true. For example: "My crystal is programmed with the energy of abundance, and I have $10,000 in my bank account now. Thank you, thank you, thank you, and so it is." After you say your prayer or incantation, see a beautiful golden light traveling from your heart into the crystal. When the golden light has filled the crystal fully, imagine a pink light coming back into your heart and infusing every cell of your body with crystalline magic. Know that you are connected to this crystal, and you will be guided to divine abundance by working with your gem.

You can keep this crystal on you (I keep it in my bra), or you can keep it by your bed, on your desk, or on your abundance altar. If you feel the need to power up your crystal, you can repeat the same richual or just leave it on your altar overnight to recharge. Do whatever feels best for you.

When you are finished working with your crystal, you can clear it with an herbal smoke wand or spray, or you can leave it to cleanse under the full moon.

Refreshing Your Altar

Refreshing your altar is a deeply devotional practice you can implement as part of your altar work. I recommend cleaning the space and sweeping away any dust or ashes once a week. If you are like me, there will be wax from burned candles everywhere. You can choose to leave leftover wax for a magical feeling, or you can scrape it up. If you have left flowers, food, or drink offerings, this is the time to switch them out for new ones.

The more you tend to and care for your altar, the more magical it will be. Some people get into a meditative state as they clean and rearrange their altars. Let your inner magic guide you to what your altar wants to look like and feel like. If you feel like putting an extra crystal on your abundance altar or making any other additions or changes, then do so. Follow your inner guidance, as it's your soul talking to you.

How Often Should You Work with Your Altar?

Some altars are created to celebrate a specific season or holiday, like Beltane and the winter solstice. Since you are creating an abundance altar, it can be active year-round and worked with whenever you desire. You might want to add something extra during major holidays to use the energy of the season to amplify your intentions.

Dedicate yourself to working with your altar at least once or twice a month. You can add some new moon and full moon richuals during those times, or maybe an opening and closing richual at the beginning and end of the month. Or, as I mentioned before, you can light a candle daily to activate and honor the energy of your sacred space, building up a powerful vortex of abundance. However—and whenever—you decide to work with your altar is up to you. Feel your way into it and see what seems the most powerful and abundant to you.

Thursday Practice

A fun suggestion is to have a dedicated Thursday practice at your abundance altar because the energy of that day of the week is connected to the planet Jupiter. Jupiter represents abundance, luck, and success, so I always make sure to do something related to money and business that day. Oh, who am I kidding, I do it every single day!

Activation Close to an Eclipse

Another powerful time to activate your altar is right before an eclipse. I know some people believe that eclipses are chaotic and you should not do any magic during that time, but I believe that they are a powerful magic amplifier *if* you learn how to work with them and the flow of their energy. The time around an eclipse is like a portal that collapses timelines and can move you more quickly toward your goals. A solar eclipse, which happens during a new moon, is a good time to activate a new desire or goal. During a lunar eclipse, which occurs during a full moon, it's best to work on a goal that is almost finished or to use it as a time to release what no longer serves you.

When activating the timeline-jumping magic available during an eclipse, it is important to be very intentional about what you are choosing to manifest. Be hyper-focused on your desires at all times. An eclipse activation is not just a brief, fifteen-minute altar practice while you let your mind wander to other things. For the entire day, stay aware of your thoughts, dreams, and actions as much as possible. If you can do this, then you will see yourself move toward your desired results in superspeed.

Remember to focus on what you desire and not what you are lacking or don't have. The energy of the Universe will give you what you are focused on, whether you want it or not.

Travel Altar

If you are dedicated to your magic and would like to fully commit to your wealth witchery, then you will love the fact that you can take an abundance altar anywhere you go. Having a travel altar is similar to working out on a vacation: You don't have to do it, but if you have a goal that you really want to achieve, staying committed is beneficial.

For a travel altar, I recommend putting a few of your favorite magical tools in a small box or drawstring bag that you can bring with you. I like to include at least three crystals; some chime spell candles; a candleholder; matches; energy-cleansing spray, like rose, or a rosemary sprig for smoke cleansing; a tarot card that represents my intention; a card holder; and anointing oil.

When you get to your destination, pick a spot that you resonate with, then cleanse the space and set up your mini altar. If you want to light a candle as part of your travel altar, please make sure that you are allowed to do so first; some hotels do not allow guests to light candles.

Sometimes, when I am on a trip, I will find something magical in that location that I can add to my altar, such as a pine cone, a leaf, or any number of things. The item itself is not important. What is important is setting an intention and believing that you are magical, that you are the creator of your world, and that you are dedicated to manifesting all of your abundant desires.

A travel altar

If, after reading about all of the ways you can put together an altar to support your manifestations, you are excited to get to work creating your altar, I am so happy for you! Working with a space dedicated to your intentions is a portal to wealth and abundance. This practice will elevate your spiritual experiences and change your life.

If you are super resistant to setting up your abundance altar, then guess what? Getting past that resistance will change your life. It also means that you should probably set one up anyway. Similarly, if you are resistant to spending time on your practice, you may make excuses such as "I don't have the time" or "This is too much work." I have said these things myself. I firmly believe when this occurs, it indicates that I am ready to ascend to the next level in my life and experience more of what I want to create; my survival brain—the ego—is reacting to the changes and is trying to protect me. The same is true for you too. So, really, having these feelings and thoughts is great! It means you are right on the cusp of your transformation! To make it over to the other side, do the thing that you don't want to do or are afraid of doing. It really is that simple.

If you want to have a complete wealth witchery practice, having a sacred space, such as an altar, is an integral part of its success. If you want to change your life, then you need to change your thoughts, habits, and actions. Incorporating positive, high-vibe practices and focused intentions into your everyday life will help manifest abundance. Have fun curating your abundance altar—it is a portal to infinite possibilities!

YOUR WEALTH WITCHERY PRACTICE

The purpose of cultivating a wealth witchery practice to be a rich witch is not just to have all the money in the world. It is about creating abundance in all areas of life, and it's about giving back as well. Being of service can look like many things, and one doesn't have to be an entrepreneur, coach, or healer to help people. No matter what your profession, it can be impactful to others. For example, a teacher can be living their best life and helping the community through enriching the minds and souls of each of their students. Hairdressers share their magic by listening to their clients' problems and helping them gain confidence by having beautiful hair, which can help them feel true to themselves. There are many ways to spread magic and wisdom, just as there are many ways to fulfill your purpose in life.

The reason why wealth witchery is focused on money and wealth is because I believe we need to have our needs and desires met *before* we can show up as our highest selves for others. When we are lacking and struggling, it is much harder to help others as successfully. When we are living in abundance and overflow, we can share more wealth—in more ways than one—with those around us.

In this chapter, I will be sharing how you can get into the flow of money, why it's important to give your money a purpose, how to receive more money, ways to let go of abundance blocks, and the Four Realms of Manifestation, which will help you discover your own unique way of manifesting.

Four Realms of Manifestation

In my twenty-plus years of studying and practicing the manifestation of abundance, also known as wealth witchery, I have discovered that there are four realms individuals must engage with and invoke as part of a manifestation practice to be able to get what they want consistently. The four realms I believe are the secret to masterful manifestation, including the creation of an abundant life, are the mental realm, the energetic realm, the emotional realm, and the physical realm.

There are many systems and programs that only focus on one or two of these realms, such as mindset or energetic manifestation. I mostly worked with the mental and energetic realms for a long time. While I did in fact manifest, I have found that once I added in the emotional and physical realms, my magic became much stronger, and my manifestation became almost instantaneous.

Mental Realm

Working with my mind and my belief system helped me move from eating ramen noodles and Happy Meals every day to getting a well-paying job and eating fresh, healthy food. When I was poor,

I had a scarcity mindset and needy thoughts and beliefs. It was very hard for me to think like a wealthy person because I had been programmed to think from a place of lack. Nobody taught me how to make money, save money, or manage money—I had to learn it all for myself. The mental realm, for me, is where the real manifestation magic began.

You see, an individual's reality is created from the beliefs in their subconscious mind. If you have a belief that money creates greedy, evil, rich people, then even if you want more money, you won't get it, because the subconscious mind and the ego (which is your protector) will keep you from having money so that you don't become greedy or evil. Even if your conscious mind wants to make more money or save more money, your ego will reject money because it is trying to keep you safe.

The mental realm requires you to release negative thoughts and self-sabotaging beliefs that can hold you back from reaching your goals. It is a reprogramming of the subconscious mind and the ego. The ego doesn't know that what you want is better for you—it just knows that where you are now is comfortable. Instead of fighting with the subconscious mind and ego, you can work with them and use them in your favor.

Think of your subconscious mind like a computer; if you download a program on a computer, the computer runs the application without you having to tell it how to do so. You don't need to think how to breathe because your subconscious is already programmed to do it. Without having to think about the step-by-step process, you can easily breathe, talk, and move around. Your mind is so magical! You can leverage the skills you already have by programming your mind to think that it is easy to make money and that when you are rich, you will do wonderful things. When you truly believe that and hold it as a core belief, your perception of the world will change. Suddenly, you will see more opportunities appear for yourself. Your brain will find ways to make sure that making money is easy without you having to hustle or work so hard for it. The mental realm is a powerful piece in the overall manifestation of what you desire.

Anything you want starts with an idea. You cannot create something if you can't think it or imagine it. Therefore, the mental realm is also about being extremely aware of what you are thinking, doing, and being. If you think there are limits, then there will be. In truth, the only limits you have are the limits that you put on yourself. In my world, I have clients that are doing what they love, working three to five hours a week, and enjoying days where they make up to $111,000. There are coaches I work with who are experiencing million-dollar months. There really is no limit to what you can manifest in your life!

The only limits that exist come from your mind. You may experience fear, self-doubt, negative self-talk, and self-sabotaging beliefs. Everyone gets these types of beliefs, no matter how much money they have or how successful they are—it is normal. The difference is how you respond to those beliefs. The question you have to ask yourself when you notice these types of limiting beliefs creep in is "Will I choose to allow myself to stay stuck in these beliefs, or will I choose to do something about it and shift out of these thoughts to get to my success?" I already know you are ready to shift because you are reading this book! Every action has a cause and effect, and just by the intention you have shown in picking up this book, you have already created shifts in your life.

Your success is inevitable. It is already yours. This is your opportunity to figure out what you want and go for it. Imagine what your life will look like once you have met your goals. Picture everything, even the breakfast you will eat when you are rich, whatever being rich looks like to you. It is important to note that there is no one thing that defines being rich. Whatever it is for you, you can create it. Denise Duffield-Thomas, a successful entrepreneur and money mindset coach, says that people often think they need a certain amount of money, or to do a specific thing that "rich" people do, in order to have success, but that is not true. Rich people are human like everyone else and make the same mistakes as a "normal" person.[4] So, it is important for you to define what being rich means to you, and remember that whatever you visualize can become real.

As I explained earlier, the mental realm is so powerful because your mind does not know the difference between what you are imagining and a memory of something that has already happened. Your mind thinks it's all real. Therefore, use the magic of the mental realm and "think" yourself to your divine wealth. Dream bigger, think bigger, and don't let anyone—not even yourself—hold you back.

MENTAL REALM MAGIC

This exercise will help amplify your manifestation powers. Close your eyes and ask yourself the following questions to tap into your mind magic: *What do I want to create in my life? Can I imagine it and see it in my mind?*

When you are done imagining your dream life, open your eyes and journal all about it. Stating it again will imprint it further. I also suggest keeping that journal someplace safe so you can refer back to when what you envision manifests in your life!

---

4. Denise Duffield-Thomas, *Get Rich, Lucky Bitch!: Release Your Money Blocks and Live a First-Class Life* (Hay House, 2018), chap. 3, Kindle.

Energetic Realm

The second realm that you get to play in as part of the manifestation process is the energetic realm. Thoughts become energy, and that energy is then sent into the quantum field to search for opportunities of the same frequency. Your thoughts create your reality, and an even more accurate statement is that what you put energy toward manifests. Wherever you direct your energy, consciously or unconsciously, that area of your life will grow and expand. If you are focusing on the thought *I have so many bills to pay*, then the Universe receives the message you want more bills to pay because you are focusing your energy on bills all the time. Instead, if you focus on how much fun you are having and believe that your bills are paid, then the Universe will bring you more of that energy. One of my clients who was learning how to manifest wanted to test this theory out, so she put her energy and focus toward manifesting free ice cream. What happened was amazing: People started bringing ice cream to her job every single day. She didn't even ask for it from anyone, and it just showed up!

When you work with magic, you are working in the energetic realm. Magic is really using energy to create intended results. The reason energy is so powerful in manifestation is because everything is energy. Even this book you are holding right now is energy. In using energetic practice to manifest what you want, the goal is to match your energetic frequency to the frequency of what you want to attract. This is similar to listening to the radio; you have to tune the radio to the station you want by changing the channel. You cannot catch the hip hop station if you are dialed into country music or the rock station. This is the same for manifesting the things you want, especially money. The frequency of $100 is very different from that of $100,000. If you want $100,000 or more, your energetic frequency needs to match that.

Each of us also has what I call an energetic container within our auric field. The auric field is the energy field that surrounds your physical body. Your energetic container can only be as big as the beliefs you have set for yourself in the mental realm. If you subconsciously believe that you can only make $5,000 a month, then that is what you will get, even if you want to manifest $10,000. To have more money and success, you have to create a bigger energetic container. Luckily, the energetic container can always expand through wealth witchery and other energetic practices!

Your energetic field is also your connection to the Universe and the quantum field. When you think of something, it vibrates through your energetic field into the Universe and connects to what you are focused on (which is hopefully what you want most) and calls it in. Combining the use and understanding of the mental and energetic realms will attract what you want even faster.

ENERGETIC REALM MAGIC

For this magical exercise, you will be checking in with your energetic container of success. First, write down the amount of money that you want to manifest. Next, write down what you are currently making, as this is where your energetic container's limit is currently set. (I like to focus on monthly revenue because it is easier to track, but you can do it however works best for you.)

Write down the amount that would be double what you are currently making, as that is the next easiest level of money energy to call in and what you can now focus on manifesting. This is an incremental step toward your overall goal and the next step to expanding your energetic success container. Trying to manifest something that is way beyond your energetic container can take a while, which may drive you toward the energy of lack or need, but if you focus on a goal that is similar to your current reality, then you will reach it faster. You will be able to build upon your new reality, expanding in additional increments until you reach your ultimate goal.

Emotional Realm

For many years, I worked with the energetic and mental realms; I rarely worked directly with the physical and emotional ones. I was able to manifest many things, but it was a slow process. The emotional realm was something I discovered about five years ago, and it was at this time that I saw a shift in how quickly I was able to manifest what I wanted. I believe focusing attention on this realm made a huge difference.

In the emotional realm, the focus is on how you feel, especially the feelings connected to your heart. If you are familiar with energy work, then you may have heard the phrase *electromagnetic energy*. This describes the energy of your auric field. *Electro* refers to your brain, as your brain creates electricity. *Magnetic* refers to your heart, because your emotions create a magnetic attraction to the things that you want. The easiest way to understand it is this: Your thoughts create electrical charges and produce chemicals that result in your feelings. These emotions then create magnetic charges and, together with your thoughts, produce the electromagnetic field that is connected to the quantum field, which holds infinite possibility.

Think of your feelings and emotions as energy in motion. Dr. Joe Dispenza, who is a best-selling author and speaker on quantum manifestation, shared in his book *Becoming Supernatural*, "When we think a thought, those networks of neurons that fire in our brain create electrical charges. When those thoughts also cause a chemical reaction that results in a feeling or an emotion, as well as when a familiar feeling or emotion is driving our thoughts, those feelings create magnetic charges. They merge with the thoughts that create the electric charges to produce a specific electromagnetic field equal to your state of being."[5] The energy goes out and connects to the thing that is in alignment with those thoughts, and the emotional energy from your heart pulls that thing in, creating your reality. Again, it doesn't matter if the thing that aligns with your thoughts is something you want—it will be called if you are focusing on it consciously or unconsciously when you have emotions attached.

Success is high-frequency. When you have more energy, you register at a higher frequency and attract better things into your life. That is why many of the magical practices that I am sharing in this book are centered around raising your frequency to connect with success and wealth. To raise your frequency, you can focus on emotions. Emotions vibrate at different frequencies. When you are happy, your frequency is raised; when you are sad, it is lowered. This is why so many books and teachers talk about being "high vibe" when referring to success and creating what you want. David Hawkins, a renowned psychiatrist, physician, researcher, and spiritual teacher, shared the Map of Consciousness in his book *Power vs. Force*, as well as how emotions correlate to the energy field. For example, the energy level of shame is at 20 and serenity is at 540. He says, "At the levels below 200, the primary impetus is survival, although at the very bottom of the scale—the zone of hopelessness and depression—even that motive is lacking."[6] In that state of

5. Joe Dispenza, *Becoming Supernatural: How Common People Are Doing the Uncommon* (Hay House, 2017), chap. 2, Kindle.

6. David R. Hawkins, *Power vs. Force: The Hidden Determinants of Human Behavior* (Veritas Publishing, 2013), chap. 3, Kindle.

being, a person's only focus is on surviving, not thriving. We have to raise our emotional frequency to change what we attract and to change our reality.

Some of the emotions and feelings that vibrate at faster frequencies are joy, freedom, abundance, excitement, happiness, and (my favorite) the feelings associated with being a winner. You will find that certain emotions have more of a charge for you. You should select one of those emotions to align to the feeling of manifestation. If you don't know which emotion to choose, the feeling of gratitude for what you have and what you will be receiving is always a very powerful energy to use because it will tap into forgiveness, understanding, and reverence, which are high-powered emotions according to the Map of Consciousness. In my experience, and in my clients', gratitude vibrates at a very high level and is one of the easiest emotions to tap into.

In wealth witchery, I don't ignore lower-vibrational feelings and emotions or refer to them as being "bad." Emotions and feelings such as fear, anxiety, anger, and sadness are there for a purpose. If I do refer to an emotion as negative, it just means it creates a negative charge and can potentially block you from what you want to manifest because its frequency does not align with what you are trying to create in your life. When you experience these lower-vibrational feelings and emotions, they could actually be your inner guidance trying to tell you that something is wrong and you need to figure out what it is. It is never good to shove these feelings down or push them away because they will most likely continue to build up, possibly exploding in unproductive ways. Lower-vibrational emotions often show up to get your attention or because something is being released so you can better align with your goals. As you release lower-vibrational emotions and call in upper-vibrational emotions, you will attract your desires.

EMOTIONAL REALM MAGIC

What high-level emotion or feeling is your superpower when it comes to manifesting your goals? To find out which one or two emotions are your superpower, state the following emotions out loud:

- Joy
- Freedom
- Abundance
- Excitement
- Happiness
- Success
- Forgiveness
- Understanding
- Reverence
- Gratitude

Which of them lit you up, especially in the area of your heart? If you have another positive emotion or feeling that resonates that is not on this list, you can certainly use it.

I want you to focus on the one or two feelings you have chosen as you are doing your manifestation activities, such as a visualization or a spell. You will be using your chosen emotion(s) throughout this book to charge your rich witch magic. It is also best practice to stay in that emotional state whenever you can. You are human, so your emotions will go up and down, but if you can stay in higher-frequency emotions throughout the day, then you will see more miracles and opportunities come your way.

Physical Realm

The final realm, which I discovered more fully and learned to integrate only a few years ago, is the physical realm. I was having trouble reaching my goal: making $20,000 per month via my business. My daily manifestation activities, which utilized the other three realms of manifestation, had helped me reach $15,000 revenue months, but I couldn't get to that next level. I worked with a sound healing coach who helped me figure out I was manifesting from my third eye and crown chakras. I was working with the other three realms, but I was not grounding my manifestations in physical reality.

I spent some time thinking about why that was. I believe the reason I didn't focus on the physical aspect was because of my upbringing. When I was little, my mom would put me in extended time-outs in a room by myself if I did something wrong. Sometimes, I was in time-out for such a long time that I fell asleep. Since I couldn't leave the room, I would get out of my body, and I would play in other energetic realms with the faeries and the unicorns. Those experiences taught me to create from outside of my body because it felt safe and fun.

While I was doing work in the energetic realm, I was not integrating it in my body. The body is the framework we have in order to be able to experience and live life on Earth. When you embody all the work you are doing in the mental, energetic, and emotional realms in the physical realm, you can consistently create the life that you desire, and you will see it manifest in tangible form. When I began working more intently with the physical realm, I began to better understand the meaning of the word *embodiment*. I used to hear that word all the time and always thought I was already embodying my magic, but I really wasn't yet.

To fully become a masterful manifester, you have to bring everything you are creating in the other realms back into the body and your physical reality. If you don't bring your manifestations back into your body and integrate them, then you will have inconsistent manifestation results. We live in a three-dimensional reality, so you have to ground the higher-level energies and manifestations that you are working with in the body.

After you visualize what you want in the mental realm, expand your energy to create it in the energetic realm, and connect to how you will feel once your intention has been manifested. Then, you can integrate it into the physical realm by noting all the practical things that will change in your life. For example, if you already made that million dollars, what actions would you take in your daily life? How would you dress? How would you walk, if you already had it all? What would you invest in? What would you eat? Any decisions, big or small, that you can see yourself making once your intention has manifested will get you closer to that future timeline. Then, one day, you will realize you truly are there in real life.

PHYSICAL REALM MAGIC

Try this simple magical exercise today. Ask yourself, *If I was already the highest-level version of myself, the one who has it all, what would I wear?* Then, put on a piece of clothing that is similar. This will bring what you were thinking in the mental realm into the physical realm because you are taking action in your physical reality.

Next, walk around like the rich witch that you are. Feel that you have already accomplished your goals—feel it fully in your body, in how you move and how you carry yourself. You might find from this point on, the next-level version of yourself wants to wear different clothing than you would normally wear on a more regular basis.

That's because you are already shifting. You are not the same person! The higher-level version of you makes different choices and gets to have different things. When you make decisions as your future self, you are one step closer to what you want.

All of the realms work together to support the same goal and intention. If your thoughts and beliefs are great but you are not embodying them in your physical reality, that will slow down your manifestation process. If you are taking action but your feelings and emotions are tied to lower-vibrational energies, then you will have to work harder for your goals. This doesn't mean that you won't receive what you want—it simply means that you might have to give more attention to the area (or areas) not in alignment. On the other hand, if you can lock in your intention and have all four realms in sync with it, you will see momentum, opportunities, and miracles show up for you every day.

While all of the Four Realms of Manifestation are significant, there really is no wrong or right way to work with manifestation. It is always about finding what works for you. Most people discover a specific realm that works best for them. I have two: the mental realm and the energetic realm. It just feels fun to work with these realms, and it's easy for me to implement them in my practice.

Now that you have an awareness about the Four Realms of Manifestation, you can move on to the next section, in which I share the basic framework of my manifestation process.

The Richcraft Manifestation System

This is the proven 21-Day Manifestation Method that is part of my money manifestation program. I have taught hundreds of clients my method, and the feedback I receive is how easy and fun this is. Many of my clients still use this method after working with me for several months. It is a must for them to do this every single day because they have seen massive shifts in their lives. I have confidence that you will create epic manifestations if you make time to do these practices too.

There are five steps in this system that, if followed, will ensure your energy is free of distractions and your magic is completely focused on your goals. This process will involve using the manifestation magic of repetition to train your brain to see opportunities and circumstances that will help you reach your goals. These five steps include invoking the Four Realms of Manifestation, allowing you to access your highest manifestation potential.

I have found that it is best to do this practice after waking up as a way of setting the tone for the day. Also, our minds and energy are fresh when we have just woken up, and they're more open to reprogramming for success. Some of my clients who have kids are too busy in the morning, so they find time throughout the day for their practice. See what works for you. There is no right or wrong time of day for this practice.

The key to the Richcraft Manifestation System is to do it every single day to reprogram your mind and create new habits. If you are an experienced manifester, daily work may not be necessary, but if you are new to manifesting or if manifesting is not working for you, I strongly recommend you do these five steps every day. Regardless of how things are going for you or your background with manifestation practices, the more consistent you are with these steps, the more quickly you will see results!

In the beginning, you might not think you can follow the Richcraft Manifestation System every day because it is too much work. Trust me, I know from experience—that used to be my belief too!

Once I put aside my excuses about how I had no time and committed, showed up, and did the work, my life started to change. Everything seems like work until you make it a habit. Over time, this practice will just be something you do every single day as part of your routine, like taking a shower or brushing your teeth.

Step One: See It

One of the most common roadblocks to manifestation is not clearly knowing what you want. If I were to ask you "What does your dreamiest, most opulent life look like?" what would you say?

If you are not quite sure, you are not alone. Many of my new clients have been known to say "I would be wealthy" or something similar. When I ask them to define what being wealthy looks like to them specifically, they have trouble answering. If you don't know—with clarity—what you most want to manifest, then the Universe doesn't know what to give you.

Therefore, step one is getting clarity on exactly what it is that you want so you are able to actually picture it. You have to be able to see the end result, meaning you have to be able to fully envision what your future self is doing and experiencing once you get the thing (or things) you most desire. Throughout this book, you will hear me say this over and over again because visualization is very important. Your brain operates in metaphors and pictures, so if you can communicate to your brain in this same way, then you can manifest what you want!

To get started, establish a daily practice that begins with step one. Tap into the mental realm by listening to guided hypnosis or meditations focused on creating the future that you desire. Write in your Wealth Journal (you will learn about this in chapter 8), and visualize your future as if it is already happening. Visualizing your future is a very important step and should be done at least once a day.

In my own practice, I wake up ten or fifteen minutes earlier than I need to. I turn on some kind of manifestation meditation or affirmations to start my day. I have a few recordings that I created in my money manifestation program that I use, but there are also great recordings on YouTube. I visualize my future by sitting or lying down in a quiet place, focusing on my breathing, and then imagining my future reality as if it has already happened. I stay in this visualization for at least three minutes; if it feels good, you can stay there for as long as you want. The most important thing during visualization is to feel high-level emotions like happiness, freedom, abundance, and joy.

If you fall back asleep, that's okay, but next time try sitting up instead of lying down so you stay connected to what you are visualizing. It is my belief that falling back asleep indicates there was some deep healing that needed to happen, and the conscious mind needed to be out of the way for it. Trust that whatever happens is for your highest and best good.

Step Two: Believe It

Beliefs influence actions, which in turn influence results. If you want to change the results showing up in your life, then you need to change the actions you are taking. To change the actions you are taking and create new habits, or patterns of behavior, that will help you achieve the results you want, you need to rewire your beliefs. Remember, you can only manifest what you believe can happen for you. This is directly tied to the Four Realms of Manifestation, and each realm has to be connected to this new belief system.

When you work on your beliefs, it is important to take a look at what is supporting your manifestations and what is not. Uncovering your beliefs is a very enlightening process, and it's not too complicated. Ask yourself, *If I had to share beliefs I have about money/wealth/business, what would they be?* Grab your journal and answer this question. You don't have to spend too long on this step; even writing down one to three things that pop into your mind is enough. Put pen to paper and keep writing until you feel finished. Don't judge what you are writing—just let it all flow. Some days, you might not have anything to say, and that is okay; simply move on. This daily practice is to train yourself to be aware of what your subconscious mind is thinking.

Go back and reread what you wrote. What resonates for you? Cross out the statements that you no longer want as part of your belief system so you can move toward the new experiences you are working to manifest. (In the next section, I will share how to release these unwanted beliefs that no longer serve you.)

Updating your belief system is not a one-time process. This should be integrated into your life periodically, and more frequently when you are in the process of focused manifestation on wealth building, as we are always being influenced by new beliefs from the people around us, social media, television, and more.

Another helpful tip for keeping your beliefs in alignment with what you want to create is to hang out with people who have the beliefs you are striving to have yourself. This may include your friends, your family, an online group, or even a coach. The more you share your beliefs and affirm them, the stronger they get. What if the people around you have a wealthy life because they have the belief system that supports it? When you are around that kind of energy, you will start to believe that it is possible for you too. When you are anchored in a belief system that supports all you want to incorporate into your life, and when you believe it is possible for you, your brain starts to look for the evidence of that in your life.

Step Three: Release the Old, Create the New

Now that you have a better understanding of how your beliefs may have caused energetic and mental blocks, it is time to release the beliefs that no longer serve you. In this section, I will teach you to clean up your frequencies so that your connection to receiving what you most want to manifest will be cleared. In order to do this, you will be taking all the beliefs that you don't want and changing them into beliefs that support you. You see, when you clear out your outdated beliefs, they leave behind an empty space. If you don't fill that space with something you want, then it will fill up with whatever gets there first. In manifestation, you are not just hoping things will happen and leaving it up to someone else—you are a powerful decision-maker and creator.

There are many tools and techniques to alchemize your beliefs and clean up the energy surrounding ones that no longer serve you; this is just one of them. To take the next step toward releasing your old beliefs and inviting in new ones that serve you much better, take the list of outdated beliefs that you made in step two, then physically rip that list up and throw it away. You can do a burning ceremony if you have time for it, but be mindful of safety anytime you are burning anything, and do not leave any flames burning after your burning ceremony is complete. As you rip up the paper or burn it, you may wish to say something to yourself, such as "I fully release these beliefs now, forever, in all time and space, and so it is." I like to do a burning ceremony once a month and on the other days, I just rip up the list and throw it away as a physical representation.

Once that process is complete, it is time to establish the new beliefs you want to incorporate. On a new piece of paper, write down the beliefs you want to replace the old ones with. These beliefs should align with the intentions you are wanting to create.

Then, carry this paper around with you, or place it somewhere you will see it daily, ideally multiple times per day. One idea is to take a picture of these new beliefs and set them as the lock screen image on your phone. For the first three days (or longer), you could set an alarm to go off every hour and recite these beliefs. The important part of this is to keep repeating these new beliefs you are incorporating until you truly believe them just as much as you believe the sun will rise tomorrow.

If you have been working with energy or your mindset for a while, then you will know when something feels off and you need a tune-up. If you are a beginner on this magical journey, then I would check in with your beliefs consciously, and practice being aware every day. Don't just let your thoughts run away on their own; take notice of everything you are thinking.

A powerful awareness practice that you can do monthly, maybe on a full moon, is to write down everything you are thinking, saying, and even posting on your social media over the course of twenty-four hours. The next day, scan what you wrote to see if there are repeating beliefs and patterns that you want to change.

Step Four: Feel It

You know from the Four Realms of Manifestation section that the emotional realm is what draws in your manifestations; your emotions and feelings are the magnet attracting your desires to you. Earlier in this chapter, I asked you to lock into the high-vibrational emotion(s) that will most powerfully call in your new reality. If you haven't yet completed that process, please do so now.

Next, follow these instructions to specifically connect your feelings to your new beliefs and your intention.

1. Choose one emotion you identified previously that resonates with you in regard to the life you want to create.

2. Take a few breaths and really breathe this emotion in and out of your heart. Notice how you feel all over when you do this.

3. Think of the new beliefs you have created and how this feeling connects to that.

4. After you have felt this feeling throughout your entire body, send the emotion into the Universe. Imagine a soft smoke leaving your heart and rising into the sky.

5. Continue to radiate this magnificent energy every time you visualize your future, at least once each day. Every time you activate the emotion and feel it in your heart, you are pulling in your manifestations at a faster speed.

Step Five: Embody It

There are several ways to embody your magic and ground your manifestations in your physical reality. One of my favorite magical practices for embodiment is to walk around for five minutes or so as if I am already the highest-level rich witch version of myself. I usually walk around the house or in my yard. During this time, I pay close attention to how I am feeling and infuse it into my walk. This can be done at any time or at multiple times throughout the day; personally, I like to wrap up my morning practice with this magical exercise.

Another way to embody your magic is to eat what you would eat as the rich witch version of yourself, or even dress the way you think you would dress if you had manifested everything you want. Though your style may stay the same, the highest-level version of you may wear different clothing and/or different accessories than you do now. The following paragraphs will help you discover some of the attributes of the wealthy you.

Close your eyes and envision yourself after you have manifested everything you desire. See how your body moves in space. Notice what clothes you are wearing and how you wear your makeup, if you want to wear any. What accessories are you wearing? Are your fingernails and toenails painted, and if so, how do they look? How do you talk, and how do you treat others? Pay close attention to everything that you are imagining, including your surroundings and the smells and sounds around you.

When you are finished visualizing, physically get up and move your body like you did in your imagination. Do this for five minutes or longer. The next time you get ready, remember how you looked in your visualization. Envision this reality for yourself. Begin to look and act as you did in your visualization, and surround yourself with the things that you saw. Repeat this practice often until you are seeing your visualizations show up in your life as your physical reality.

If you imagined something that you cannot afford yet, that is perfectly normal—you do not have to go out and buy it. Instead, you can take the first step toward it. For example, walk into the store and imagine yourself buying that thing you visualized. Just being in the store and using your imagination can be very powerful.

And remember, it's not just about the material things. Envision the actions you saw yourself taking as the highest-level version of you. How will you interact with others? You might not feel called to behave that way now because you are not that version of yourself yet. However, a way to shift your mindset and embody your future self is to ask yourself one simple question. When you are going to take an action, ask yourself, *As a rich witch, what would I do?* Whatever answer you receive, do that.

All of the magical practices in the Richcraft Manifestation System will create new neural pathways in your brain, connecting you to the life you want and the person you want to be. The more you invoke that new identity, the more your experiences become the reality you desire. These embodiment practices are not just something you do once—they are meant to be practices you include in your daily life. For example, sometimes when I'm shopping for groceries, I walk around tall and proud as a rich witch, and I say to myself, *Wow, I am shopping and I can buy any food I want to enjoy. I am a millionaire!*

Have fun with this and practice consistently embodying the life you desire. From now on, take full responsibility for what you are choosing to believe, do, and manifest. You will notice that if you start focusing on what you desire instead of scrolling through social media, you will have more time in your day. Be responsible for the life that you are creating and your results. If you show up and do the work, you will be rewarded.

Things will open up for you if you are consistent. Maybe not immediately, but you will start to see your life shift. I worked two jobs while trying to build my business and writing my first book. I still found time to do my magic, and it was the driving force to succeeding in my goals. Energy is the most important thing because we are all energy, and everything you want is energy. Now, I spend one to two hours each day on my wealth witchery practices because I know how important it is for me to be aligned with the frequency of what I desire. If you add the simple and potent Richcraft Manifestation System into your daily life, this practice will lead to experiences beyond your wildest dreams.

FIVE

LEVEL UP YOUR
RELATIONSHIP WITH MONEY

Are you ready to love money and have money love you? This magical concept is one of my favorite things to teach to my manifestation students. Many of the clients I coach who are trying to manifest more wealth in their business experience immediate shifts after they change their relationship with money. Get ready to discover more about how you really feel about money and how money feels about you. What you are about to read is going to change your life! Creating a good relationship with money is a must, whether you want to impact the world or just live your very best life.

Money is an important part of our society, whether we like it or not. It makes the world go 'round. It is the energetic currency we have chosen on this planet, and it allows us to get things that we want. The more money we have, the more experiences we can have. So, in this chapter, you will be doing a meditation to meet your money so you can build a better relationship with it.

Just a reminder before you go on this journey of uncovering the truth about your relationship with money: Whatever your current relationship with money is at this moment, it is okay. It is divine timing you are here right now, reading this book and taking action. Don't ever feel like you are not good enough or like you are behind just because you see others ahead of you. The truth is, it's impossible to know how much work other people have done internally and externally to get to where they are. Actually, when what you are focused on manifesting for yourself starts to show up for the people around you, then you know that it is getting closer to you!

It is also okay to want the things others have, because that means that whatever you are envious of is really your desire as well. I love to celebrate others' wins and genuinely feel happy for them because I always think, *If they have it, then so can I!* Turn the feelings of jealousy around and see them as a possibility portal. If you see someone who has what you want, then just know it is possible for you to get it too. Anything is possible, and you can manifest whatever you want. You are figuring that out right now!

Before you meet your money, I want to make sure you enter this magical journey with positive beliefs. First, I'm going to share my core beliefs about money, which have allowed me to keep manifesting money and build wealth. These are beliefs that you can borrow if they resonate with you—and if they don't, that's okay too. Just know I paid a lot of money to be coached by some seven- and eight-figure entrepreneurs who know how to manifest massive amounts of money, and some of these beliefs are ones that I've borrowed from them. A few of these beliefs were already mentioned in other chapters of this book, but that's because they have served me well and been very powerful in my life (and in the lives of my coaches and clients), so I really want to pass them on to you.

As you continue to read this chapter, you may find it hard to accept some of the things I've written. It's also possible that what I've written will spark major aha moments for you. Maybe it will be a little bit of both. Whatever your reaction, it's what you need at this point in your journey. Just be willing to keep going and try the magic that is being shared.

Money Belief #1: Money Is Important

I rate money as one of the most important things in the world. It allows us to get the best things in life and to experience more freedom. I've had this debate with many people, and they have said things like, "Well, isn't health more important? Because if you aren't healthy, then how can you enjoy your money?" While this is very true, if you had an unlimited amount of money flowing to you, then you would be able to prioritize your health. Perhaps you would eat the freshest, healthiest foods, pursue the best medical care, work with the best trainers or healers, or live in a clean environment with alkaline water. Having money can help prevent some illnesses, and if you did get sick, you would be able to afford the best medical treatment out there.

People have also asked me, "Aren't relationships more important?" Some people believe that having all the money in the world would be pretty boring and lonely if there was no one to share it with. My response is "Get a pet." Just kidding! In regard to relationships, money can help you access a variety of amazing places and opportunities to meet many different people, including those with similar interests and those who are also living their best life!

To be clear: This belief is not all about making money. Rather, it is about being abundant, which to me means living a holistic life in which all areas of life bring me wealth. Let's flip it and think about it this way: Some of the clients I have worked with got a divorce because of money challenges. If their relationships had experienced less financial stress, they would have been able to focus on growing and expanding their relationship instead.

In my opinion, thinking that money is not important, or having distorted views of what it means to have money, is why many people don't have money. If someone thinks money is unimportant, they won't give it much thought, attention, or focus. Due to those beliefs, the energy they put toward generating money will be minimal or ineffective, and their results will reflect that. I know there are all kinds of reasons people don't think money is important. Most likely, it has to do with things that were taught to them or events they experienced when they were young, especially when they were eight years old or younger—during that time, we are sponges and soak up everything around us. Perhaps your parents were trying to protect you because they did not make a lot of money and wanted you to worry less about what was happening, so they told you things like, "Money isn't important. Love is what matters." As you grew up, that would then be programmed in your subconscious mind as "Money isn't important." Consequently, whenever money did have the opportunity to come in, it may have ended up blocked by that subconscious belief even if consciously, you knew you wanted more money.

Most people aren't even aware that this thought is part of their belief system and end up thinking they are fine being where they are. If that sounds like you, great, but if you are reading this book, I bet you have big dreams and want so much more! If you resonated with that limiting belief, don't worry—everything that you are reading in this book will help you clear these kinds of beliefs to bring in more wealth and abundance. You already started doing this work in chapter 4!

Before moving on to the next section, do this quick exercise: Write down all the reasons why money is important to you and what you could do with money.

Money Belief #2: Money Can Bring Happiness

Most of the people who tell me that money can't buy happiness don't think money is important. They don't believe in the value of money and what it can do because they either haven't experienced it themselves or they have had negative experiences with money. They may have felt screwed over by money in some way; perhaps they got into credit card debt. I am guilty of that! In the past, I ignored money because it made me upset to look at my bills.

The truth is, money can't buy happiness because happiness itself is not a tangible thing that can be bought. Money *can* buy the things that make you happy, including paying for the things you want without stress. Money can also buy a safe, comfortable place to live. Money can take you on your dream vacation. Money can buy your kids clothes and toys that make them—and you—happy. Being happy is a powerful energy and emotion to embody because it invites in more abundance and success. If you start to attach happiness to money, then you will be able to attract more of it.

Do you want more happiness and fun in your life? If so, write down three things that money can buy that would put a smile on your face right now.

Money Belief #3: Money Does Not Make People "Evil"

This money belief is one that most people struggle to believe. You may have seen articles about some of the richest people in the world making poor decisions or doing bad things. This is partially because the news likes to report the bad things people do rather than the good, because bad news gets more viewers. There are plenty of rich people doing good things with their money too!

So, you might have seen how awful some people with money are as well as all the things they are doing with their money. This might create the limiting belief that money makes people evil. This belief could also be a subconscious programming if you were told this when you were little; it may have been passed on generationally from others around you. In any case, this limiting belief means your subconscious mind may be repelling money and keeping you from being wealthy because you don't want to be evil. This belief may even be to blame if you struggle to hold on to money. You may be able to manifest money, but when it comes in, this programming will kick in, leading to self-sabotage and quick spending.

Money is a piece of paper, a coin, or a credit that we exchange. Like everything else on this planet, money is made of energy. It is up to the person who owns this energy to direct it. If the energy (money) from one person is making bad things happen in the world, then it is the person who is directing the money that is to blame, because they are not acting with good intentions. It is not money that is evil or mean. A truer statement is, "Money makes you who you are." When a person has money, they get to be the fullest expression of their soul. They get to be anyone they want to be! This expression will be negative or positive depending on the person whose energy is directing the money. If a person is already evil, then money will just make that person able to do more evil things. If a person is heart-centered and caring, then money will allow that person to do amazing charity work and help the planet.

Increasing your wealth can help you more fully express your authentic self. Say you want to give back to your community and donate to a local animal shelter because you love animals; this will cost money and/or time. If you have no money to donate or no time to spare because you are working multiple jobs just to pay your bills, then you will not be able to show up as the fullest expression of you. See, money is amazing and allows you to do so many things, like donating to charities to save animals and trees around the world.

Ask yourself, *If I had an unlimited amount of money, how would I use it to even more fully express who I am?* Grab your journal and write your answer to that question. Dream big!

Then, take a moment to check in with yourself and see how you are feeling at this point. Are you ready to go deeper and uncover more possible blocks within you, or do you feel you have clarity and are ready to move on? If you feel ready to move on, then you can skip the rest of this section. If you feel there's more to release, answer the following questions, writing down whatever comes to mind.

- How do you really feel about money?
- What are some negative thoughts or feelings you have about money or in regard to making money?
- What are some negative experiences you have associated with money?
- What are some negative beliefs that you have because of things you heard or saw others doing with money? Do you have any negative beliefs because of things you yourself have done with money?
- What is currently blocking you from your money goal?
- What is your current relationship with money?

As you reflected on some possible money beliefs, different emotions may have surfaced, and that's okay. Just let the feelings come up, and let yourself feel them fully. This is part of the process of releasing the energy attached to those beliefs.

Money Dynamics

Now, it's time to learn even more about who you are in relation to your money so that you can shift into a healthier dynamic and create a more positive relationship with it. As you go through this section, you might wish to refer to the reflection questions you just answered to make further connections. Wherever you are in your relationship with money, or whatever is currently in your bank account, don't beat yourself up. It's important to be extremely honest with yourself about how you currently see yourself.

In this section, I am sharing some dynamics that you might unconsciously be holding on to. Some of these beliefs and dynamics cannot support you on your rich witch journey. As you read, pay attention to which (if any) of these dynamics feel true for you. Then, throughout the next few chapters, as you are reprogramming your mind toward wealth, you can release the dynamics that are holding you back.

Ghosting Your Money

You don't like to look at anything having to do with numbers and money, even though you do want to have more money in your bank account. This especially includes bills (which may or may not be sitting on your desk right now), which stress you out.

The Struggle Is Real

You haven't had the best luck with manifesting money, even though you can manifest everything else.

Emergencies Only

You are able to always manifest money, but only at times when you "need" it.

Hot Potato

Money—sometimes a lot of money—appears in your life and you feel so blessed, but you can't seem to hold on to it. It is like playing hot potato. Saving money is a struggle for you.

The Number Witch

Oh, you love numbers! You love looking at your bank account and counting every penny that comes in. Your money looks and feels good, and you are ready for more.

Comfort Zone

You are satisfied with your financial status, but you are curious. You want to get out of your comfort zone and grow even more. Maybe you have a good career, but lately you have felt called to take risks and change jobs or start your own business.

Dripping in Gold

You have a constant flow of money coming in and are successful. Congratulations, rich witch! You have accomplished so much and have acquired divine wealth. Now, you are looking to ascend to the next level of riches and manifest beyond your wildest dreams.

Were you able to see yourself in one or more of these money dynamics? All of this information will be helpful as you move toward creating your new relationship with money. Truthfully, I have had each of the money dynamics in this section, especially before I started my own business.

If you want to be dripping in gold, you have to have an amazing relationship with money! Being "okay" with money isn't enough, because you want to achieve your wildest dreams, right? Rest assured, you are already doing more than others may be doing simply by reading this book. As long as you are committed to change and taking action, then you will manifest more of what you want in your life—and in your bank account.

Meeting Your Money Meditation

In this magical meditation, you are going to discover how money shows up in your life right now. Then, you will transform your current relationship with money so that money loves you, wants to come to you, and will stay with you. The goal is to create an amazing, safe, and trusting relationship with money so that it will continually flow in and support you in every way. Money is just energy represented as a piece of paper, and now you are going to channel that energy!

Step One

Grab the journal that you have been writing your reflections in so you can add to it after completing this section. Then, settle in a comfortable spot and close your eyes. Relax in your seat. Focus on taking deep breaths that fill up your belly with each breath in, and fully release with every breath out. Repeat this a few times.

When you are ready, bring your awareness to the black space behind your eyes. In this space, you will meet your money, which is based on your current relationship with money. To do this, bring up all of the thoughts, emotions, fears, and beliefs that you have about money. Allow yourself to fully feel all that comes up, then gather the energy together. Give it a form. It can be a person, a blob, a light, a monster, or anything else it wants to be, but it has to be an actual thing you can visualize. What you have created is your money, and it is important you make it as real as you can.

Notice what your money looks like, how it makes you feel, and perhaps how it feels if you can envision touching it. Also notice if it gives off a smell, because usually it smells really stinky and has a foul odor. It's okay if you feel really uncomfortable with your money at this moment—that is part of the process.

Take a moment to tell your money how you really feel about it at this moment and why. When you are done noticing your money, you are ready to move on to the next step.

Step Two

Now, it is time to tell your money that you appreciate all it has done for you, but at this point, you are ready to move on to create a more loving and abundant relationship.

Place your hands on your heart as you think about how you would feel if you had an unlimited amount of money coming into your life, an amount of money that guarantees everything you want will be taken care of. How would you feel if you could do anything and have anything you want? Tap into the feelings of love, gratitude, joy, and any other high-vibrational emotions that are coming up for you, including those superpower emotions you connected with previously.

Gather that feeling in your heart space and imagine it as a beautiful pink and green light. Then, stick out your hand and point your palms toward your money. Visualize sending this pink and green light to your money. Imagine this version of your money being covered by your energy. See your money start to blur and shift. Your money is now shifting into your new money.

Step Three

Your new money emerges from your beautiful cocoon of pink and green light. Using the same concept as you did in Step One, give your money a new persona. Create a money that lights you up and brings a smile to your face.

Who is this new money for you? What represents the money you can completely love, trust, open your heart to, and receive unconditional love from? What does your new money look like? You might see a celebrity or someone you know in real life, and that's okay as long as you feel excited about meeting them. What is your new money wearing? What does it smell like or feel like? My new money is a buff dragon shape-shifter, usually wearing gladiator-like armor, who has lavender eyes and blue hair. You can get as creative as you want! Just let your heart guide you.

Your new money is your energetic soulmate who exists in the quantum field. It is ready to connect with you and shower you with abundance and wealth. It is a relationship you will need to work at and evolve into. Eventually, you will easily connect to that frequency in order to draw your new money in. Your new money is here to help you clean out, balance, and untangle past money blocks and open your heart to divine wealth energies. Your new money has the utmost respect for you. It is filled with unconditional love and wants you to succeed!

Step Four

Once you have created and made contact with your new money, ask, "What is it that I have to do, or shift, in order for more money to come into my life and for you to stay with me?" Allow your new money to answer, as it will tell you exactly what it wants from you or what you can do to expand the wealth in your life and align with your goals.

Receive the answer your new money has for you. If you don't think you can do what it has asked yet, or if you would like to do something differently, then negotiate with your new money. Have a conversation with it and learn what you can do to make both of you feel loved, safe, and part of a beautiful, *rich* relationship.

Step Five

When you are done spending time with your new money and figuring out the actions that you can take to manifest more money, thank your new money. You can give your new money a hug if you feel called to do so. Know that you can come back to your new money—which now represents all of your money—to chat whenever you want. When you are ready to close this meeting with your money, all you have to do is bring yourself back to the darkness behind your eyes and connect to your body and your conscious awareness.

When you are ready, open your eyes and write about your experience. As you write, include what your next steps will be based on this experience and the information you received. My favorite part about teaching this visualization to my clients is when they share details about their experience with me. If you want to share with me, direct message me on Instagram @pamelaunicorn. I would love to read about your money magic!

That's it! Isn't connecting to your money this way fun and easy? Your money is there for you whenever you need it. All you have to do is close your eyes, bring the image of your money into focus, and start talking.

If you had any trouble "seeing" your money, that is normal for most beginners. However, the more you practice, the more your clairvoyance, or visual intuition, will sharpen. For now, you might not be able to see your money, but can you hear it? Do random pictures or words pop into your mind? Those are all messages from your money. Sometimes the messages are not clear; that is normal too. A lot of times our money just gives us clues, and it's up to us to put them together and figure out what they mean.

No matter what your initial experience was, keep opening yourself up to this new relationship with your money, and have fun with it! In the next section of this chapter, you will learn how to continue building this relationship.

Money Dates

Yay, you have alchemized the first version of your new money! No matter what your experience has been with this process so far, you can continue to develop this relationship further. Most importantly, like any relationship, it needs your attention. You don't want to ignore your new money, because then there is a good chance it will turn back into the money you had a negative relationship with, and you don't want that!

I previously shared that I used to ignore my money. I would never look at my bank account or the bills that were coming in. At that time, looking at money was scary for me, which of course prevented more money from coming in. After I took responsibility for what I was creating and the money that was flowing in and out of my life, I began to pay off my credit cards, bit by bit, and to manifest more money in my bank account. I learned to love money in all forms—not just when I was making money, but also when I spent it.

When I started my business, one of the accountants I spoke to (who was also really magical) told me to set up money dates. I listened, and money dates have completely and positively changed my business. Having a money date is really easy: All you have to do is schedule a day of the week to have a date with your money. A money date could be three minutes or thirty minutes, whatever you decide. During this magical time, you can do whatever you want as long as it is associated with money; you could organize your finances, pay bills, or whatever needs to be done. The one thing that you should commit to as a rich witch is meeting your money during this money date.

Make this money date something you look forward to doing every week. I recommend setting up your money date so that you feel excited to spend time with your money. This will look different for everyone. You could light candles, do a spell before, play beautiful music, burn some incense, dab on some essential oils, have your crystals surrounding you, or drink something yummy. If you would like more structure, there is a beautiful Monday Money Richual that can be used with your money dates in chapter 10.

When you are meeting with your money, you can have a picnic and talk about how the week went or what you need to feel supported with everything that is going on. If something is not feeling good for you or your money, then talk about how you can make it feel good. Perhaps ask what actions you need to take, or what beliefs you have to change, in order to stay in an abundant flow of money. Ask your money if there is any advice that could help you reach your money goals.

Having a weekly money date really changed the way I felt about money and manifesting money. It made the whole process fun! I started to love money, talk about money, and make more money. So, before you do anything else, plan your money date. I highly suggest you have your money date on the same day every week so that it can become a ritual. I like to do my money dates on Thursdays because that is the day of the week associated with the planet Jupiter and abundance. You could also consider Fridays because Friday is ruled by the planet Venus and represents love. A lot of the students in my manifestation course like to schedule their money dates on Mondays because it's the start of the week and they feel it's a good day to get everything in order, including their money.

You should also be mindful of the time of day you schedule your money date. Is there is a specific time of day that you prefer, or a time of day that feels more magical to you? For example, some like to schedule their money dates at 11:11 as they feel more aligned to magic at this time. What is most important, like everything else, is to see what works for you.

Before reading further, pick a date and time for your first money date and write it in your calendar now. Even setting this up will help shift things in the right direction. Love your money, and your money will love you.

SIX
PROSPERITY
DREAM BOARD

A prosperity dream board is a vision board for abundance. It is simply a visual anchor of images and words that represent your intentions and goals. Your dream board is a visualization of everything you want to have, be, and do. The images you choose to include on your prosperity dream board should make you feel motivated and inspired to reach your goals. A prosperity dream board is a powerful magical tool that can allow you to subconsciously reprogram your mind; the objects and images on your board will spark your brain to find the opportunities and actions that match what you are calling in. It is a reminder that the possibilities already exist for you, and it's all about aligning your thoughts, beliefs, and actions to receive them.

Having a prosperity dream board also helps you get clarity on what you want to create and which direction you are headed. Life gets busy and we can get off track, so having a solid reminder of what your goals are can help you stay focused.

While creating your dream board is a potent way to manifest anything that you desire, it's not just about slapping a bunch of pictures on a board. Though it is one of the easiest and most fun ways to tap into wealth witchery, you don't even need to believe in your prosperity dream board! I am going to teach you how to make and use a vision board that actually works to manifest your dreams. All you have to do is follow the instructions in this chapter.

Before starting your prosperity dream board, make sure you have read chapter 4 and have a crystal-clear understanding of your goals. Next, decide whether this dream board is going to represent your long-term vision or your short-term vision. You can always make two boards if both timelines are calling you. I personally like to represent long-term goals so I feel extra supported and like I have enough time to manifest my desires. When I create dream boards for short-term goals, I feel rushed and anxious. However, a good friend of mine is the opposite. She loves short-term goals because she can create immediate plans to manifest, and the long-term goals seem too far away for her. There is no right or wrong choice. Just be in your magic and see what feels good for you, which option excites you most, and which option resonates for you.

An additional magical tip—and something I discovered was life-changing for me—is to include visuals and images of what you already have on your prosperity dream board. Use pictures, drawings, or words to represent the abundance in your life, especially anything that you have already manifested for yourself. This will be the bridge to help your mind connect where you are to where you want to be. Your mind likes familiarity, so it will find comfort when it sees the images of what you already have; plus, your subconscious mind won't be able to tell the difference between what is real and what is not manifested yet. Remember, your mind does not know the difference between what you are imagining and what is a real memory. It all is real to your mind, which is why visualization is so powerful. Creating a prosperity dream board will also prep your inner system for change, allowing you to easily manifest your intentions.

The next step is to pick a place to put your images and words. Prosperity dream boards can be any size and on any material, paper, or board you choose. Maybe you only have a piece of paper—that works! Or you may be someone who wants to get a huge cork board and pin everything to it with golden thumbtacks. Thanks to modern technology, you can even make your dream board on your phone or on your computer. I have three digital prosperity dream boards, and I have one set as my phone's lock screen, one as my phone's background, and one on my computer, so I see them every single day. I'm not a techie, but I found creating a digital version to be very easy. Create your dream board in the way that makes sense you. This is a very unique and personal craft just like your magic, so your dream board does not need to be like or look like anyone else's.

How to Create a Prosperity Dream Board

First, I will share the steps for creating your prosperity dream board physically, on a board or paper, and then I will dive into how to create a dream board digitally. These are the practical steps for creating the actual board. After reading this section, I highly recommend making your board during a Prosperity Dream Board Ceremony, which I will discuss later in this chapter. A Prosperity Dream Board Ceremony can really accelerate the manifestation process and create amazing energy to aid in the manifestation of your desires.

Dream board

Crafting Your Dream Board Physically

1. Decide what material you will be creating your dream board on. Once you have your board, craft all your images and words, print them out, or cut them out of magazines or newspapers. Have these images and words nearby, ready to be pasted.

2. This step is optional. Write your intention in the middle of the board, but write as if it has already happened. Imagine you are already at that future date, reflecting on the past. For example: "It is [DATE], and I am so happy and grateful that I've already manifested $100,000 into my bank account."

3. Start to arrange your words and images on the board (or whatever you have chosen to use) in ways that feel and look the best to you. I recommend not adhering anything yet; wait until you have a solid idea of where you want everything to go. Have fun with this step, knowing that as you create, your energy will be infused into your board.

4. Once you know where you want the images and words on your dream board to go, stick everything to the board using glue or another adhesive.

5. If you'd like, you can then add stickers or other fun additions to make the board come alive.

6. Once you have finished gluing and decorating your board, put it somewhere you will see it every single day at least a few times. Even better, put it somewhere you will see it for longer periods of time, like next to your bed, in the bathroom, or in your office.

Crafting Your Dream Board Digitally

1. Decide which device you want to put your prosperity dream board on. Is it your cell phone, tablet, or computer? I recommend creating your dream board on a device that you use at least once a day.

2. You can use an app or website to create your digital dream board; there are several free options. My favorite one to use is called Canva. It's really easy: You just save photos that are related to your intention, drop the photos into a collage, and then save this graphic on your device. There are other apps that can do this too; use the one that is easiest for you.

3. Set your digital dream board as the background on your device so that you look at your goals every time you use your device.

Prosperity Dream Board Ceremony

Crafting your prosperity dream board as part of a ceremony is optional, but it allows you to manifest your board in a more devotional way. Being in ceremony activates a reverent energy around what you are doing and sends a message to the Universe that you are serious about creating what you desire. It also creates a deeper connection to your board.

This is the simple framework that I created for my personal Prosperity Dream Board Ceremony. You can follow exactly what I did or switch it up.

Step One

Light your favorite candles, cense the space, diffuse essential oils, and gather all your favorite crystals before starting your ceremony.

Step Two

Prepare a favorite drink. I like to open my ceremonies with a high-vibe drink to activate my physical body. Matcha is my go-to magical beverage because it tastes good to me, balances out my energies, brings the joy of life into my entire being, and increases my spiritual awareness. If you are more of an earth or kitchen witch, you might want to use cacao. Cacao activates the heart center and creates expansion through that area. Both drinks are an amazing way to start off your ceremony. If you do decide to drink matcha or cacao, make sure to buy pure matcha or cacao, not versions that have additives in them. Also, when you drink something for a ceremony, always drink it straight—don't add sugar, milk, or anything else to it. This ensures the beverage's energies are potent.

While you are stirring and making your drink, be very intentional. Think about what your goals are and the magic that you are creating through your prosperity dream board. Then, consume your beverage.

Step Three

Center yourself and get grounded in your space. Take deep, expansive inhales and long exhales. As you do, intend to release anything that is not serving you at this time, and let go of all the stress and energy that may be separating you from your goals. Focus on being in your magical, radiant energy. Take as much time as you desire.

I like to imagine a golden iridescent light emitting from my heart and surrounding my entire body, and as I breathe, I focus on expanding it as far as I can. Sometimes I like to incorporate crystal magic with this step, and I will either surround myself with crystals or hold a crystal while I am breathing.

Step Four

Once I have activated my energies, focused on my goals, and placed myself in the present moment for my ceremony, I like to journal. One recommendation is to use the practice in chapter 8, Writing Your Rich Reality, and a Wealth Script related to your Prosperity Dream Board.

Step Five

Start arranging the images and words that will be on your prosperity dream board, either physically or digitally, as outlined in the steps provided in the previous sections.

Step Six

Before you put your prosperity dream board somewhere you will see it every day, you should activate it. Hold your hands over your dream board and state your intention out loud three times. Then, imagine your dream board and intention being wrapped up in a golden ball of light, the very same light that surrounded your body in Step Two. Take a large breath in, and in an upward swooping motion, as if you are lifting the energy of the board up, send your golden ball of light into the Universe, followed by a powerful exhale.

To really lock in your goals, visualize yourself accomplishing all of the things you've put on your prosperity dream board. Use your senses to make the visualization as real as you can: See your manifestation coming true, hear what you are saying to yourself and to others once it has, feel the emotions you are experiencing in this new reality, taste the celebratory dinner that you are eating or perhaps something you are drinking, notice anything physical that is happening, and notice the smells you experience as you envision it all. Incorporating your senses in visualization creates a more tangible reality for your brain and helps facilitate manifestation in a powerful way.

Now, your prosperity dream board is ready to be displayed.

Step Seven

Your dream board manifestation doesn't just end here, with the creation of a board. Magic and energy work are only part of creating success with your manifestation. The next magical step is to take inspired action that aligns with your goals and intended results.

Again, take action with the attitude that you have already achieved and manifested everything on your dream board.

As preparation for inspired action, reflect on the following questions as the version of yourself who has already created the results:

- What were the actions I took to accomplish my goals and to create what I wanted?
- What were the steps I took that were the most powerful and helped me manifest what I wanted quickly and in the best way possible?

Take a moment to journal about your responses to these questions, writing down whatever comes to mind. You already know the answers deep within you, so let yourself write freely. If you need more guidance, you could fill in the following blanks: "I am already_____, and the actions I took to get here were _____."

Keep writing as much, or as little, as you like. Even if you end up writing something unexpected, like drinking matcha, be open to taking that inspired action! This is actually how I found out that matcha is a high-vibrational wealth witchery drink, which, as I have shared, has helped me create more abundance in my life. The actions you are guided to take may be surprising to you, but reaching your goals does not always happen in ways you thought about previously; sometimes inspired action is about doing the things that put you in a state of abundance so you can be on an accelerated path.

After you've finished journaling your responses to the previous questions, write down the next three actions you are going to take based on the information you've discovered. Then, get out there and do those things!

Step Eight

To truly embody what you most desire, it is important to connect to your prosperity dream board at least once a day or, even better, multiple times a day. If you look at your dream board before going to bed, it could inspire your subconscious mind to think of ways you can get closer to your goals while you sleep. If you look at your dream board in the morning, it could help you focus on what you want to feel, be, and attract that day and also motivate you to achieve your goals. The more you look at your dream board, the more likely your mind will take you to those opportunities, and you will begin to attract opportunities into your life.

As you move forward and continue referring back to your dream board, it can be helpful to ask yourself what your next inspired action should be. You can ask this question daily, weekly, or monthly.

Updating Your Dream Board

As you grow and evolve in your magical practices and in your life, your goals will too. If you tend to experience shifts really quickly, then you will need to update your prosperity dream board more often. Personally, I like to reconnect with my goals every three months and decide if I need to change things up on my prosperity dream board. Determine if everything on your board is still in alignment with your goals based on how things have evolved. If your board is no longer in alignment, update it accordingly. You could make a completely new dream board and start from scratch, or you can swap out some images and words for new ones.

If some time has passed but your prosperity dream board still represents what you want, continue doing the work, applying the practices in this book, and envisioning your intentions becoming reality.

I know many people who like to create a prosperity dream board every year. This becomes its own richual. Create a new dream board on the first day of the new year, whenever that is for you based on your own traditions. This way, you are updating your prosperity dream board at least once a year. Ultimately, it is up to you to be aware of when you are ready to modify, expand, or recreate your board.

Prosperity Dream Board Circle

When I discover something super magical and amazing, I like to share it with all of my friends, family members, and clients. If you are like me, then you may want to do the same. One way to do this is to share the act of creating a prosperity dream board with others in your life. Can you imagine if all of your loved ones were living their best lives with love, magic, and joy? How amazing would it be if everyone in the world was practicing their magical craft and showing up as the highest and best version of themselves? If you feel inspired by what I just wrote, you are welcome to consider this aspiration a part of your purpose too.

One way to start making this dream a reality is to gather and share the magic of the prosperity dream board with people in your life. If you feel called to do so, you could invite some of your best friends to a prosperity dream board creation circle or gathering. This is just another way to put what you want out there and amplify your manifestations. It's also very powerful when a group comes together to work magic. Vision boards are very popular, and they are actually used by many companies in a non-magical way, so this concept is not too "woo-woo" for most people.

I did a mini dream board manifestation ceremony with a friend of mine in Hawaii. It was very last minute, so it was not set up the way I would've liked, but my friend and I wanted to use the energy of 2/22/2022 to magnify our intentions. So, we worked with what we had, and we did it together. We lit a candle, got out some crystals, and drew and wrote our intentions on a piece of paper. I would say it was a success, because my friend was able to manifest her biggest goal within a month! Manifesting and doing magic with others is so powerful, and it is also fun. If you want to take your prosperity dream board to the next level, then share it with your BFFs!

How to Host a Prosperity Dream Board Circle

1. With intention, choose who you want to make magic with and invite into your circle. Depending on how open they are to working with magic, you could use very witchy words to invite them, or you could keep it simple and say something like, "Hey, I'm hosting a vision board party where we'll focus on the goals we want to manifest. Would you like to join me?" You can invite as many people as you like! If you are a coach or mentor, you can even charge for this and host it online instead of in person. If you are hosting it online, it is easiest to set up a Zoom meeting and have everyone bring their own items.

2. Decide whether or not you will be doing the Prosperity Dream Board Ceremony as part of your gathering.

3. Select a date and time for the gathering. I like to work on a day that represents something "new" to me, such as a new moon or New Year's Day. The day before the gathering, I suggest sending out text reminders.

4. If you are meeting in person, have everyone bring supplies, whether they bring magazines, glitter, or something else they think they'll want to use—and share, if possible. As the host, I recommend providing the basic items (board, scissors, glue, etc.) to be sure there are enough for everyone. If you are going to be incorporating the Prosperity Dream Board Ceremony, provide matcha, cacao, or another beverage that everyone will drink. You can also make the gathering into a potluck and have everyone bring food and drinks in addition to their supplies.

5. Once everyone has gathered, make sure they have clarity about their intentions and goals. You can have everyone share their goals and claim the manifestation of what they most desire, if that would fit for your group. Then, you can all begin crafting your dream boards using the instructions provided earlier in this chapter. If you have decided to perform the Prosperity Dream Board Ceremony, follow the steps provided, or customize the ceremony based on your preferences and the group you have. If you are doing the ceremony or something similar, it is important to make sure that everyone is on the same step of the process to ensure the powerfulness of the group manifestation container.

6. When everyone is done with their dream board, you can do a sharing circle. Ask everyone to explain the images and words on their prosperity dream board and state their intentions again.

7. After everyone is finished, you can go your separate ways or stay and hang out. I recommend hanging out as a group if you have time—this is a great opportunity to keep talking about your goals as if they already manifested. You can stay

in that magical vortex during your time together and even afterward by staying in touch and celebrating each other's wins!

As you can see, prosperity dream boards can be a powerful tool for your wealth witchery practice. The creation of your prosperity dream board and the words and images on it will make your desires clear to your subconscious mind. Your brain will believe that the things on your dream board are meant for you, and there will be less resistance from your ego during the manifestation process. To keep your brain and subconscious mind engaged in creating what you most want, connect to your dream board often (at least daily) and remember the most important part of the process: taking inspired action!

SEVEN
RICH WITCH
SOUL ESSENCE

The quickest way to manifest the reality you desire is by changing the way you feel, think, and act, which is your identity. The version of yourself that you desire to be—in this book, I call it your *rich witch self*—is made up of your personality, habits, and beliefs. It is an internal programming that projects into the physical realm and creates your reality. That is why it is so powerful to create change at the identity level first, before trying to change the environment.

Here is a more in-depth example that illustrates the difference between changing your environment and changing your identity. On New Year's Day, many people make New Year's resolutions, and a common resolution is to get in shape. So, in January, most gyms are packed. In February, gyms are still busy, but a little less so, as some of those New Year's resolutions have already gone by the wayside. By March, gym attendance is back to the way it was before January. Why? Well, most people that made the resolution to get fit only changed their external actions and their environment; they didn't change their soul essence, their identity. When shifting at the external level, a person may buy new gym clothes, maybe a new water bottle. They'll start eating healthy meals and going to the gym on set days each week. They are determined to feel their best and be their best self. However, despite the best intentions, using will-power alone to force change is hard, and most of the time it does not work out. Past programming takes over, and there is a gradual reversion to who someone believes themselves to be, including the habits they most identify with. Therefore, if a person identifies with wanting to relax all day, then that is who they will ultimately revert back to if they haven't done any internal work to shift this identity. A person's outer and inner world need to match for long-term success. Changing the external world is important for expansion, but inner transformation must occur too.

What if you changed how you identify with yourself first? What if you started changing your beliefs, thoughts, actions, and habits to become the person you want to be? Those who start from the inside out, working on being the energetic match to anyone they desire to be, have a higher success rate than those who only change their environment and focus externally. In this chapter, you will be learning exactly how to be a successful manifester by shifting internally first. You will be tapping into the soul essence of who you are currently and learning how you desire to express yourself—including your rich witch self—in order to create the life you most desire.

Discovering your rich witch essence is an important part of your wealth witchery practice. In the next chapter, you will be provided a framework and an opportunity to connect to this version of yourself. The work in this chapter will be the foundation of your wealth manifestation practice, as it focuses on the deep inner work of becoming your most authentic rich witch self. This is a very powerful transformational process; I've seen clients immediately manifest more money and happiness in their lives just by using these techniques.

Crafting Your Rich Witch Identity

You can be anyone you desire to be. Your potential is limitless. Whatever you can think of in regard to manifestation can also become part of your everyday reality. The key is to create internal shifts that make sense to your brain and that you believe are achievable. It is important to note that everyone is different, and the level of change that each of us experiences will be different as well. Some people can manifest extreme change in their life very quickly and find stability within the life they have created at a rapid pace, but others do better with incremental changes.

When you are crafting your rich witch self, it's important to focus on who you want to be in life and all that goes along with that. Your ideas can be a bit of a stretch, but they should be achievable. Your intentions must be something that, at some level, you believe can happen for you. It is okay to manifest your new reality in increments because refining and adjusting is always a part of life, and you want the changes you shift into along the way to really take hold with results; I tend to shift and up-level every few months. When you achieve a goal or move toward it significantly, you begin to see what the next expansion is and dream even bigger.

It's time now to take out your journal and craft your rich witch life. Start by looking at areas of life, imagining that in each of these areas, you are overflowing with abundance:

- What are the things you are saying to yourself?
- What are your beliefs?
- What are you wearing?

- What do you look like?
- How do you walk and stand?
- What do you listen to?
- What do you read?
- Where are you living?
- Who is around you?
- What do your relationships with friends, family, and romantic partners look like?
- What do you not tolerate anymore?
- What does your work, job, or business look like?
- What are your hobbies?
- Where do you go on vacation?
- What do you do every day?
- How much money do you earn?
- How much money do you have in your bank account?
- What does your spiritual, personal, or magical practice look like?
- How is your health? What does your body feel like?
- What is your impact and influence on the world?
- What do you invest in?
- What organization(s) do you donate to?
- What does your average day look like?
- What are the rules of your world?
- What are you committed to?
- What do you value?

Feel free to add anything you would like as long as it resonates as important in this process.

Visualizing Your Rich Witch Self

Complete your identification of your rich witch self in as much detail as possible. This is important, as it lays the foundation for this wealth witchery practice. You will need to know, with clarity, exactly who you desire to be and how you want to show up in your life before moving on to the next section of this chapter. Soon, you will connect even more deeply to this version of yourself through visualization.

Wealth witchery frequently works with visualization as a manifestation tool. Visualization is when you picture, or imagine, something in your mind's eye. In this chapter, you will use visualization to imagine your future and your future self. When you activate your imagination and work with visualization, you are also using one of your intuitive powers called *clairvoyance*. There are four main intuitive powers that most people work with: clairvoyance, which is clear seeing; claircognizance, which is clear knowing; clairsentience, which is clear sensing; and clairaudience, which is clear hearing. When you visualize the rich witch version of yourself or the future, you will mostly be tapping into clairvoyance, but it is okay to use other intuitive powers that you are familiar with or knowledgeable about.

When visualizing, not only do you want to see the future playing out in your mind, but you want to be able to hear what's going on, feel what's happening, and maybe even smell or taste something. The more details in your visualization, the more senses you can activate, and the more your brain will believe it to be real. This is how you can reprogram your mind to manifest the abundance you desire. You are consistently sending imagery to your brain, and your subconscious will search for opportunities to make it real. With this magical technique, you won't have to work hard because you will be programming your subconscious mind to do it for you. This is how miracles happen—things just start to show up in synchronicity, like magic!

When I share this concept with a group, there is typically someone who tells me they cannot "see" or visualize anything. I have learned from working with clients that there is a very small percentage of people who can't visualize or imagine anything. I have only had one client so far who truly could not visualize, even with practice. When they closed their eyes, they saw nothing but darkness, even if they were doing a guided visualization. If you think you can't visualize or see anything at this time, that might be a limiting belief you've had, or it might be because you were never taught how to visualize. Both of those are easy fixes.

Now, let's see if your mind's eye is open, and if you are able to visualize and imagine things. Do this mini exercise:

1. Close your eyes and imagine a red apple.
2. Now imagine a pink unicorn eating the apple.
3. Erase the picture of the apple and the pink unicorn and open your eyes.

Were you able to imagine the apple or the pink unicorn in your mind? It might not have been crystal clear for some of you, and that's okay. As long as you saw an image in some way, shape, or form, then congratulations! Rest assured, your visualization magic is powerful. You will be able to visualize your future and much more.

Practicing visualization daily will strengthen your magic in this regard. I was not born with strong visualization skills, nor have I ever had an out-of-the-ordinary experience to open up my psychic vision. However, clairvoyance is one of my most potent intuitive powers now, and that is because I have practiced daily for quite a long time. Practice imagining things and daydreaming to boost your clairvoyant powers. The more you visualize, the more clarity you will receive.

For those of you who did not see anything, don't worry; there is another way to tap into your future. Instead of clairvoyance, you can rely on other intuitive powers. You can amplify and connect to the emotions or physical sensations in this future version of you. You can also connect to the thoughts that are running through your head as the rich witch version of yourself. You may even be able to connect to sounds that resonate as you think of your future self. There are many ways for you to connect to what you most want to manifest, even if you struggle with visualization. With that being said, if you were able to catch even a glimpse of that apple or pink unicorn, I want you to continue to try to visualize and "see" your dream life. If you were able to see anything at all, that means you have the ability to visualize, and all you lack is practice. Visualization is like a muscle: As you exercise it, you strengthen it.

Rich Witch Name and Symbol

This visualization process can help you embody your rich witch self, the future version of yourself that has everything you desire. I have found that doing my best to stay connected to the energy of my rich witch self allows me to manifest faster and more frequently. During this visualization, you will be receiving a symbol and a rich witch name; both of these things will allow you to consistently connect to this magic.

My rich witch name is Pink Cotton Candy. That's because when I visualize the rich witch version of myself, the feelings and the smells are soft, pink, and puffy, like cotton candy. Your witch name may be a more mundane name; one of my client said her rich witch name was Maggie, like her mother, which we all thought was so beautiful.

The symbol you receive will immediately attune you to the future version of yourself whenever you need to tap into that frequency; it is like a button you can press that is anchored to your rich witch self. Your rich witch symbol might be something that you are familiar with, or it might be a new symbol. One time, during a group visualization with my clients, four of the women in the session had the same heart symbol. It was a very interesting class to say the least! My rich witch symbol is always some form of a star. I like to upgrade my rich witch self whenever I create new intentions, and my symbol almost always changes. However, my rich witch essence stays the same, because it is aligned to the feeling of me living in my joy and aligning to my magical purpose.

When you reach the part of the visualization where you receive your symbol, allow whatever wants to show up. Though it might not be the symbol you want, or a symbol that you don't relate to at this time, honor your magical symbol anyway. Trust that it is the right one for you at this moment. With time, it may evolve and change (like you!), but for now it is the symbol that represents this part of your journey.

Sacred Symbol and Rich Witch Visualization

Now, it is time to visualize your rich witch essence in meditation. The easiest way to deeply enter a meditation is to record yourself reading it aloud all the way through, then to play the recording back when you are ready to take the journey. That way, you don't have to keep opening your eyes to read during your visualization. Please note, it is important to record the meditation exactly as it is written because it is coded with magic and positive mindset language.

Also, it is helpful to know that in one part of the meditation, I will guide you to start walking so that you can embody your rich witch essence in your physical reality. Therefore, before getting started, please make sure you have room to walk and move around.

All right, let's do it! Get ready for some magic! See you in the quantum realm!

> *Sit back and relax. Gently close your eyes and breathe deeply, in through your nose and out through your mouth. Good. Keep breathing deeply as you sink deeper into your seat or the ground beneath you. Your whole body is relaxed, and you feel like a heavy blanket is covering you. Rest assured that you will be safe and supported on this magical journey to connect to your rich witch essence and sacred wealth symbol.*
>
> *Next, focus on the darkness behind your eyes. Directly in front of you, a beautiful door appears. Go ahead and open this door and step through it, knowing you are protected on both sides.*
>
> *When you are through the door, you see that you are in the most beautiful space. It might be a field with flowers, a waterfall, or even a castle in the sky. Wherever you are, it feels amazing and powerful. It feels like home. Somewhere in this space is where your rich witch essence lives.*
>
> *As you look around this gorgeous place, you see something glittering out of the corner of your eye. You quickly walk toward this sparkling light, and when you get there, you see that it is a treasure box. The treasure box is gold*

with beautiful jewels all over it. You sense that something special is locked inside.

You suddenly become aware that you have pockets, and you notice your left pocket feels a bit heavy. When you reach into your left pocket, you pull out a matching key to unlock this treasure chest.

You insert the key and turn it gently. Click. The treasure chest suddenly opens, and you see a symbol resting on a pillow. There is your rich witch symbol and your rich witch essence. What is your symbol? Notice what shape it is and its color. Then, notice the energy of your essence.

Your symbol suddenly sparkles and wants you to pick it up. You pick up your symbol and hold it to your heart. Next, you take a deep breath in and out through your heart center. Every time you breathe in, you are merging with your essence. Continue breathing until the symbol is fully embedded in your heart and the energy of your essence is surrounding your energy field. Breathe in deeply and slowly until you are one. Good.

As this rich and magical essence of yourself, notice how amazing your body feels. Notice the feelings in your heart and how your energy has changed. See if you can feel how your body has shifted. Maybe now you are sitting up taller than before, with your shoulders back. When you are done noticing the changes, slowly open your eyes while continuing this mediation.

Once your eyes are fully open, feel how radiant your energy is as it projects into your surroundings and into the world and space beyond.

Next, get up slowly, and start walking. As you do, notice yourself walking in this new energy as the new you. You *already have everything you desire. As you walk, embody that rich witch who has it all. Think of everything you wanted that you now have. Notice how you are walking and how powerful you feel.*

As you walk, ask for your rich witch name. Remember whatever you hear, see, feel, or know. If your rich witch name doesn't show up for you right now, that's okay; you will receive it later. Be aware of the name or word that you are receiving now.

Continue to walk around for a little bit longer, taking each step as your rich witch self.

Return to your seat and sit back down. Close your eyes and notice how you are feeling in your heart. What is the essence, what is the energy you feel in your heart? Is it an emotion? Is it a color? Does it have texture? Does it smell like anything? Or perhaps it's just light. Whatever you feel and see is perfect for you. Really lock in to this energy, because every time you call upon this energy, this essence, this symbol, you will connect with the reality you have created.

Whatever you have experienced today in this magical space is real.

Gently return to your body and come back to the present moment. Feel the new reality you have created. When you are ready, open your eyes to a new life that is dripping in riches.

Congratulations, rich witch! Thank you for trusting me and letting me take you on this magical journey. Know that this meditation was just the beginning. Messages and more information may come to you throughout the day via songs you hear, words that pop into your head, or things showing up in your dreams. Be aware of anything that stands out to you and write it in your Wealth Journal. The secret to consistently manifesting what you want in life is to show up every day tapped into your rich witch essence and making decisions from that future version of yourself. The more aligned actions you take as that future version of yourself, the faster you will reach your goals!

Feel free to come back to this meditation any time you are in the process of further expansion. As you change, you may notice your symbol change. The symbol you received today is an anchor that can help you tap into the current frequency of your essence. You can use this symbol in many different ways, such as adding it to your prosperity dream board, drawing it in your journal, or putting it somewhere you will see it often so that you will unconsciously show up as your rich witch self every time you look at it.

In the next chapter, you will learn another powerful magical technique that can help you manifest your wildest dreams.

EIGHT
WRITING YOUR RICH REALITY

The magic contained in this chapter has been taught to me by multiple business coaches and *their* coaches, each of whom is a multimillionaire or billionaire. This wealth creation strategy, utilized by highly successful entrepreneurs and business owners, is the magical practice of wealth journaling. This is also one of the first techniques that my clients learn in my money manifestation program. Now, you will also learn and embody one of the secrets to divine abundance and success.

Wealth journaling itself is very simple; the hardest part is actually doing it. This is not a get-rich-quick scheme in which journaling one time will manifest a million dollars in the bank. While this *could* happen—after all, we are infinitely magical beings with potent manifesting powers—it won't if you don't truly believe it can be your reality. That is why an important part of this practice is consistency. You must constantly shift your energy and mindset to be the new, rich version of yourself.

In chapter 7, you tapped into your rich witch essence to discover why you want more money and who this next-level version of yourself is. In this chapter, you will be using the practice of writing your rich reality to match the energetic frequency of the future you who has it all. You will jump timelines, allowing you to manifest your abundant desires more quickly. Wealth journaling can also help you stay focused on your intentions and amplify the spells you have already cast. To truly get the most out of this practice, you have to be persistent, show up consistently, and write your rich reality to reprogram your mind, body, and energy.

If you love to journal, that's great, as this practice will take things to the next level and add another layer of richness to your craft. When I shared this powerful richual with an avid journal writer, they gave it a try. Later, they shared, "Why haven't I ever thought of this?! I am not ever going back to the old way of journaling."

If you don't love to journal, that is okay too. The first time I was taught this magical concept, I was very resistant. I was never a journal writer; I never did any of the journaling prompts in the programs I was taking. However, even though I was resistant, the idea intrigued me because this type of journaling practice involved magic, manifestation, and the creation of my ideal future. After thinking it over, I decided I was willing to give it a shot. I thought, *Hey, if it worked for my coach, then it will work for me too.* I was definitely inspired after watching her triple her income and her client base within a year.

I want to reassure the rich witches who are not journal writers that writing your rich reality is unlike the normal way of journaling. (Trust me, every time I join a manifestation course and I get bombarded with journal prompts, I roll my eyes.) This process does not require you to write down what has happened in your life, your emotions, or any details of the day. Instead, you will be tapping into your inner magic, activating your rich witch essence and allowing your wealthy self to come forward to write your future. Even if you don't like to write, you may find yourself easily writing a page or more as your magic flows through you.

Wealth journaling is a magical richual that will magnetize money, wealth, and riches to your life. To date, almost everything I have written down in my Wealth Journal has manifested unbelievably fast. One of my favorite examples to share with my clients is when I started manifesting five-figure revenue months. It was the second year of my online business, and I decided to get serious about turning my side hustle into a lucrative business. During this time, my side hustle was making around $2,000 per month, and my goal was the illustrious $10,000. That seems to be the dream number for most entrepreneurs. Since I had seen it happen for multiple people, I knew it was possible. I had the programs and system set up for it, so the question was, how was I going to make it happen?

There were critical changes I made in my business, but the one thing I was consistent with and took action on was focusing my energy and magic on receiving and having $10,000 months. I doubled down on my magical richuals during this time, and I wrote in my Wealth Journal every single day, even if I was traveling. I created my rich reality by truly believing that $10,000 was already mine. In fact, I wrote, "I've been making $10,000 for a while now, and it is normal." I wrote down the details of how it all happened and how happy and grateful I felt. Guess what? Within three months, I went from $2,000 to $15,000 revenue months! The fourth month, I had a revenue of $25,000, and money just kept flowing in in increasing amounts. This was not just luck or coincidence; rather, it was a focused intention I called into reality consistently while using all my tools, including daily wealth journaling.

Entrepreneurs can easily double or triple their income, but no matter your career field, there are ways to manifest more money in your life. I had one client who manifested a $50,000 bonus for the year from her employer. My clients see money come in so many different ways, not just via their job or business. Be open to however it will appear. You could also focus on manifesting experiences instead of money; another client of mine manifested an all-expenses-paid trip to Europe.

One of the reasons that wealth journaling works is because the process automatically puts you into a magical state of being, like we talked about in chapter 7. This instantly connects you to the flow of money and allows you to be a powerful magnet for abundance. When you write your rich reality as your future self, you are connected to the frequency of whatever it is you desire to have. You jump timelines and bring the future reality into the present reality. Even if this doesn't make sense to you at first, or you don't believe this, you can still get started and have it work for you. Eventually, you will see the results, and this will further fuel your beliefs, which will power up your manifestation results. I can't state enough what a magical cycle this is, and one that will allow you to manifest money and your desires more and more quickly!

One of the reasons that wealth journaling is highly effective is because you are speaking to your intuition and your cosmic guidance system. When you follow the wealth journaling formula, you unlock your cosmic guidance system, the part of yourself that has a connection to the Divine, to your soul, and to all the answers that exist there. You have probably felt this connection strongly at certain points of your life; you may have felt confident about something or sensed you were on the correct path. When you are wealth journaling, you are actively and intentionally allowing yourself to surrender and call upon this state so that you can clearly hear what your soul essence is trying to tell you. You have a unique soul map that can show you the easiest way to success—all you have to do is access it.

To successfully manifest your riches, you have to be connected to the magical energy flow of the Universe. If you don't hop out of bed feeling vibrationally aligned to your wealth, you have to do the work to get there. While nobody is at their peak magical level every single time they wake up, the difference between extraordinary people and ordinary people is that extraordinary people worked on themselves and didn't give up to get there. The great news is the work doesn't have to be hard or time-consuming. That is the beauty of wealth journaling! It can gracefully transform you into the future version of yourself by collapsing time to achieve your goals. What you might have manifested in four years can appear in six months.

As I stated before, wealth journaling is not just sitting down to write. There is a specific way to do it, which I am about to share with you. Before you read on, decide that you are going to commit to this fully and that it is going to work. Say, "I am easily and consistently wealth journaling every single day and massive amounts of money are flowing in to me." Better yet, shout it and dance around!

Selecting Your Magical Tools

The first step to having a successful wealth journaling practice is getting your magical tools together. You will need something to write on and a pen or pencil. I am not even giving you the option of doing this on an electronic device because there is something magical that happens when you put your thoughts on paper.

Since you are going to be manifesting riches and divine wealth, choose a journal that puts you in that energetic state. (This journal is not to be confused with the grimoire that records your magical practices, discussed in chapter 2; your Wealth Journal is specifically for manifesting and writing your riches into reality.) Your Wealth Journal could be a ninety-nine-cent green notebook that makes you feel wealthy or an expensive leather-bound journal that makes you smile every time you see it. The retail price of the journal does not matter; choose a journal that connects you to the frequency of abundance instantly. The last two Wealth Journals I chose were custom-made. A good friend of mine who is a musician and shamanic channeler downloaded a millionaire light code for me, sang it, and wrote it out in symbols. Then, another magical friend who is a master creator transferred this millionaire light code onto a black journal with the divine symbols etched in silver. However, you don't have to go all out like I did. My first few Wealth Journals were just plain green ones that cost me less than a dollar, but I loved writing in them. What you feel when you work with the journal is more important than where you got it from or how much it costs.

For your sacred writing tool, choose a pen that writes well rather than one that catches your eye. When I am writing my rich reality, I am in a magical flow. To stay in my magical flow, I need my pen to flow with me. It is the worst when I am in the zone and my pen stops working, not because it is out of ink but because of its quality. I consider it a bonus when I find super cute pens that write well; they make me really happy, which gets me even more excited to write in my Wealth Journal every single day.

Find what brings you joy and motivates you to write in your Wealth Journal daily. You could incorporate stickers, markers, or colored pens to create your visions with art.

Journal and pen

Prepping for Your Magical Writing Practice

When I was just beginning my wealth journaling practice, I found it hard to jump right in, so I developed these pre–wealth journaling richuals. I've included them here in case you feel similarly. Prepping is not a requirement for wealth journaling, and you can write your rich reality in any conditions you desire. However, finding what resonates with you—and maybe even designing your own personal prepping richuals to help you get into the right headspace before wealth journaling—can be very helpful. Read through the magical elements that I added to my practice and notice if any resonate with you.

Pre–Wealth Journaling Richuals

- Cleanse the room with an herbal smoke wand or clearing spray. Lemongrass and lavender are my favorite scents to spray.

- Burn incense that contains magical ingredients connected to manifesting abundance. This can change the energy of the room immediately. I love the smell of cinnamon, and it is one of the main magical herbs used for money and wealth.

- Burn a green or gold candle, which both signify wealth, and anoint them with some Grand Success or Open Roads oil. This is something I do quite frequently. The act of lighting the candle indicates I am illuminating the path to my success by sitting down and doing my rich witch practices.

- Select a crystal of the day and have it near you. I either place the crystal on the table next to me or in my bra. This richual puts me in a positive emotional state before I start wealth journaling.

- Choose where to write. This is very important to me. I love writing in a brightly lit place with fresh air. My favorite places to write are in my office or outside with my chickens. Occasionally, I write on the couch because I am comfortable there. Ultimately, write somewhere you can comfortably dream of your rich reality.

- Write in front of the altar you created if you need a powerful space for this process. See how you feel when you sit down with your Wealth Journal. I have noticed that when I write in front of my altar, more channeled messages from my guides flow through, and I write with more energy.

- Sometimes, to activate my magic, I like to jump or dance around to get my energy up. Doing so can release blockages in the body and move you into a space of receiving.

- Before doing any magical practice, I always wash my hands with special money soap. You can find these soaps at metaphysical shops or search online for recipes and create your own. Since much of the magic for wealth journaling is in my hands, I make sure to clean them meticulously before I write.

- Although this is not something that I practice, you can always call on the Universe, gods, goddesses, the creator of all that is, angels, ancestors, your celestial guides, or whomever you pray to and believe in. Ask them to protect you and guide you toward your highest and best good. I don't intentionally call upon anyone because I have already made it my belief that I am divinely guided and protected whenever I journal. Do whatever resonates for you.

- When I sit down to write my rich reality, I always make sure that I have a beverage next to me (usually coffee), and I take a sip before I begin. Writing and a mug of coffee or tea seem to go together in my head, so when I have my Wealth Journal and a beverage, they signal to my brain that I am ready to begin.

Wealth Journal Formula

Yes, rich witch, it's time! You are now prepped, confident, and ready to co-create a future in which you have everything you desire.

Step One: Practice Gratitude

Write down eleven or more things in your current reality that you are grateful for and why. For example, "I am grateful for my chickens because they make me laugh" or "I am grateful for my mineral toothpaste that helps keep my teeth healthy." These gratitudes will supercharge your writing and close the gap between where you are now and where you desire to be. You can repeat the same gratitudes every day or change it up; it is totally up to you.

When you are finished writing, set your Wealth Journal aside.

Step Two: Envision Your Future Self

Next, get very clear on what exactly you desire and what the future version of yourself is like. Your future self is your rich witch essence, which you discovered in chapter 7. (If you are uncertain who you desire to be, go back to chapter 7 and do the exercises, then return to this section.) In this step, you will be connecting to the energy of your future self and calling in that magic.

Once you are embodying the energy of the future version of you, visualize an amazing day in the life as your rich witch self. Spend at least three minutes visualizing. Try to visualize an entire day playing out in your imagination. When I do this, I envision the version of myself that is consistently making $100,000 a month, always flowing in with ease.

When you imagine an experience, your subconscious mind does not know the difference between that visualization and reality. It thinks that it has already happened, and so your brain will act like a magnet and align things in your physical reality to make it real. That is why being able to clearly see what your desired rich future looks like and who you are in it is very important.

Step Three: Connect to the Feelings of Your Future Self

Another magical ingredient of powerful manifestation is connecting to how it feels to be your future self. You have to feel this in your heart and in your whole body to magnetize abundant goals to you. Feeling next-level emotions is the difference between regular journaling and wealth journaling. When you write in your Wealth Journal, you're not just writing—you are deeply feeling the future as you write.

Feel what it is like to be your future self, then embody the emotions of that version of yourself now. When you are wealth journaling, you can lock into those next-level emotions and anchor them in your reality. Next-level emotions vibrate at a higher frequency, just like success and money, so you always want to choose to be in that state. For this step, you can use the same emotion you chose in chapter 4 for the emotional realm, or you can choose another high-frequency feeling.

If you don't know what to feel, then you can always feel grateful. When you are thankful for something, that tells the Universe that you have received the object of your desires, you are happy with it, and you want more of it.

Step Four: Begin Automatic Writing

Grab your Wealth Journal for this step. Now, you will be opening the channel to your future rich witch self via automatic writing, which is when you intentionally move your conscious mind aside and allow your subconscious to step in to share all the secrets of the cosmic realm. The key to automatic writing is to write down whatever comes to mind first without analyzing it. These thoughts might seem like your own, as that is how they appear to me most of the time, but they really aren't. Another way to think of this is as channeling through writing.

Approximately one out of ten students of mine doesn't get this immediately, but after a few tries, the magical downloads begin for them. Don't give up! If you think nothing is coming through, practice every single day.

I am going to share an exercise to begin channeling, tapping into your magical flow, and allowing the future version of yourself to come through. Once you have practiced enough, you won't need to do this exercise, as you will naturally be able to tune in to your next-level self and journal anytime, anywhere.

Sit down in front of your wealth journaling tools and close your eyes. Focus on your breathing, inhaling and exhaling deeply. Bring your awareness to the center of your body, then down to the base of your spine. Imagine a golden cord dropping from the bottom of your spine and extending all the way into the middle of the earth. See this cord wrap itself around a giant crystal, anchoring you to the earth. Next, travel back up this cord and into your body, focusing on the base of your spine again. Then, imagine the energetic center above your head—your crown chakra—opening up like a gorgeous flower. Envision big, beautiful petals unfurling slowly. When your flower has fully opened, call upon the next-level version of yourself, inviting that version of yourself to show up in the flower. See this energy coming in through your head and into your body. Open your eyes and start responding to wealth journaling prompts.

WEALTH JOURNALING PROMPTS

These prompts are open-ended, and they are meant to connect you to the future version of yourself as you fill them in. There are a few different options here; feel free to use them all during one journaling session or switch them out daily. Remember, just write, write, write, and let it flow!

- It is [future date], and I am consistently making [fill in your money goal] every month automatically. It is so fun and easy for me!
- The actions that I take daily are…
- The emotions that I now feel are…
- The thoughts that I now think are…
- The beliefs that I now have are…
- The things I released that no longer served me, which helped me get to this level, were…
- The important things I changed that led to me being this successful self were…

End your writing with one or more of all of these options, or something similar that resonates with you:

- And so it is.
- It is done, it is done, it is done.
- Thank you, thank you, thank you.
- This or something better.
- For my highest good and the highest good of all.
- [Draw magical symbols like stars or money signs.]

Step Five: Closing

Write until you feel complete, then close your connection to your future rich witch self. Close your eyes and come back into your body. Thank your future self for sharing their magic with you. Close your crown chakra by closing the flower that you saw opening in step four. Imagine yourself going down the middle of your body, back to the bottom of your spine. Follow that golden cord back down to the crystal anchor in the middle of the earth and unwrap your cord slowly. Gently pull back the cord into your body and ground into your physical self. Wiggle your hips. When you are ready, open your eyes and welcome the new future you have just created.

You can now read through what you wrote with your logical mind. Piece together the clues and make sense of what you wrote.

Step Six: Activate and Ground

Activate and ground your rich witch identity, energies, emotions, visions, and future reality into yourself right now. Put your hands on your Wealth Journal and feel a golden light flow from your journal into your hands. Imagine this golden light gently infusing every cell of your body and your auric field, filling you up with the riches you have just manifested. Stay in this experience as long as you wish. When you are ready, open your eyes.

Step Seven: Embody Your Future Rich Witch Self

This might be one of the most important steps, and unfortunately, it is one that most people don't take. After you read over what you have written, it is your job to embody what you have channeled. If your future self shows up a certain way, then you need to show up that way in daily life. To magically attract that future to your reality, you have to be that person, do what that version of you is doing, and feel like you already have the things you want. You can't wait until you have what you want to take action, or you'll be waiting forever!

For example, say that you can't wait to receive $10,000, which will make you feel complete, supported, and happy. You have to feel those feelings now. Via your Wealth Journal, your future self shared with you what actions you need to take every day to succeed. These are actions you must take now so that you become your wealthy, abundant self. If the action is something totally out of the realm of possibility right now, like flying first class, then try your best to take a step in that direction. You might not have the funds to buy a first-class ticket right now, but you can always research which airline has the ideal first-class seats, or you could plan where you would like to travel while flying in first class. You could even upgrade your ticket from economy to business class on at least one flight if you are flying sometime soon. These incremental steps will move your energy and reality in the right direction.

Step Eight: Stay Consistent

Repeat these steps often to manifest feeling comfortable in a new vibrational frequency of wealth. You may experience instantaneous shifts if you do this daily. If your shifts are not obvious right away, or if you don't notice any forward movement, keep showing up and doing the work. Your intention might be so amazing that the Universe is working in the background to make sure everything is in place for you. You can, in fact, live the life you most desire.

The number-one mistake manifesters make is giving up on their practice because they don't see results within the timeframe they expected them to show up. Trust, believe, and stay with it, no matter what. Continue to implement the wealth journaling practice outlined in this chapter on a consistent basis, and use the other richuals in this book to help you remain the next-level future version of yourself. When you do, the money will begin to flow.

NINE
WEALTH WITCHERY SPELLS

Spells can be cast by anyone with ease. Even though most spells call for magical tools, all you really need is an intention, though using words, actions, physical items, and/or the energies of the Universe can help you hyper-focus on your intention. I believe working with tools connects the intangible to the tangible more efficiently. When you work with tools, you are showing the Universe that you are doing something to make your manifestations real. This core belief will help fuel your intentions and speed up the manifestation process.

The spells I have created in this book are very easy, fun, and effective. They don't use any rare magical items you have to go out and buy. In fact, most of the suggested tools can be found in your home already. If you don't have something I've listed, feel free to substitute it with something that has similar energy. Remember, the objects themselves are not magical—it is the actions and intentions you attach to them that create magical results.

When you are performing a spell, do so from a grounded, clear, and focused headspace so that you can powerfully direct your mind toward your intended results. If you are performing a spell from a place of neediness or a scarcity mindset, you might get unexpected results.

Even when you follow all of the instructions perfectly, the outcome of a spell may not be exactly what you think it is going to be, so don't get too attached to the result. Always stay open to receiving what you want or something better. Most of all, try to stay in a positive mindset, and remember: Being rich is fun, doing magic is fun, and fun is the vibrational energy of success! So have fun with your practice to create what you desire!

INSTANT CASH SPELL

To successfully manifest money, you need to create an energetic space for the money to reside. It's sort of like a bank account; you need a magical bank to attract cash into your life. With this spell, you are going to easily call in instant money by creating an enchanted container for your new wealth. I have seen this magic work for my clients, who have manifested $2,000 in a week and $24,000 in three months!

Remember, spell work is not just doing a spell and watching as the money flows in. It is important to take aligned actions to speed up the manifestation process. Once you have used tools to call in your riches and set the magic of the Universe in motion, you need to create movement in the physical realm.

MAGICAL TOOLS

An herbal smoke wand, incense, or a high-vibrational spray

Petition paper

A green pen

Your favorite anointing oil

The largest dollar bill you have

Dried basil leaves

A wooden or cardboard box

INSTRUCTIONS

While you can perform this spell anytime, the best days of the week are Thursday or Friday, or during the new moon phase.

1. Cleanse your space with incense, a smoke wand, or a high-vibrational spray. Then, gather all of your magical tools.

2. Using a green pen, write your intention in detail on the petition paper. Make sure you state exactly how much money you are manifesting. I always like to add "or more" to my intention in case the Universe wants to send me even more money than I am asking for. Here's an example of an intention: "I am so happy and grateful I already have $[dollar amount] or more in my bank account."

3. When you are done writing, fold the petition paper toward you once. Rotate the paper to the right and fold it once more toward you. Then, rub one drop of anointing oil on the paper in an upward motion.

4. Next, anoint your dollar bill with one drop of oil and spread it in an upward motion three times.

5. Put the petition paper, the dollar bill, and one basil leaf into a wooden or cardboard box and close it. Hold your hands over the box and say your intention out loud as a way of infusing the box with your intent. As you speak, imagine a

green smoke leaving your hands and flowing into the box. Your spell work is finished for the day.

6. For the next three days, open the box every day and put another basil leaf in it. Each time you close the enchanted container, say your intention out loud and send energy into the box. This will feed your spell and help you manifest cash faster.

7. On the fourth day, take the money and petition paper out of the enchanted container and put them in your wallet. You can offer the basil to your garden, put it on your altar, or throw it away. You can reuse the box in future magic once you have cleansed it.

8. Finally, the most important thing is to expect money to come in. To speed up the process, think of actions you can take to bring in money, then do them! I recommend making a list of twenty ways you can call in money and taking one action every day. Now that you have created an enchanted container for money to arrive, you will encounter miracles and see cash in your bank account.

LUCKY PROSPERITY SPELL

Are you ready for a lucky break? Maybe you are down on your luck or just want a massive boost of good fortune. This is the spell for you! Luck is something everyone can experience—it is something you can create. Luck is a real energetic frequency. A little luck can go a long way, as it can lead you to new opportunities and create miracles in your life. Do you want to get a new job, sign a publishing contract for your book, or receive a bonus? All of this and more is available for you when you tap into the magic of being lucky.

When luck is on your side, things will suddenly be easier, and it will seem like offers are just showing up at your door.

In this spell, you are going to work on mental reprogramming. One of the main reasons people don't experience luck in their life is because they unconsciously believe they are unlucky. This belief is usually due to past experiences that convinced a person things do not work out for them. Does this resonate for you? In this Lucky Prosperity Spell, you are going to call upon Lady Luck and invoke her magic to encounter abundance with ease.

MAGICAL TOOLS

An herbal smoke wand, incense, or a high-vibrational spray

An offering bowl

Uncooked rice

Dried corn kernels

Seven coins

Any prosperity anointing oil

Seven dollar bills of your largest denomination

A photo of yourself

A green aventurine crystal

INSTRUCTIONS

Before you start this spell, dress in the outfit you feel the luckiest in. Wear something that makes you feel happy and abundant. This spell is all about your feelings related to luck and believing that you *are* lucky.

1. Perform this spell at your abundance altar. (Make sure there is space on your altar for the offering bowl.) Cleanse the space with incense, an herbal smoke wand, or a high-vibrational spray and gather your magical tools.

2. Put your offering bowl on your abundance altar and add rice, corn, and the seven coins. When the bowl is as full as you would like it to be, add seven drops of prosperity anointing oil and mix it well by shaking the bowl. While you are mixing, think of instances when you were lucky. For example, maybe you got a really good parking spot, found money on the ground, or just feel lucky to be alive and breathing.

3. Roll up the dollar bills you have chosen to use. Stick the rolled bills into the bowl at random. As you are placing the dollar bills into your offering bowl, share intentions that focus on one area of your life where you want to experience luck. For example: "I am grateful that I am so lucky when it comes to my business. Clients easily flow to me, and I am a money magnet."

4. Put a picture of yourself in the center of the bowl and top it off with a piece of green aventurine. Your spell has now been activated and will continue to bring you good luck each day it is on your altar.

5. To keep empowering your luck, you need to speak to it every day. At a specific time of day, go up to your lucky bowl and tell it how lucky you are. Share what has happened in your life that was so lucky. You will notice your luck building and becoming more powerful every day.

6. When you feel happy with the amount of luck you have manifested in your life and you know you have embodied luck as a part of yourself, you can remove the bowl from

your altar. I recommend keeping the coins, aventurine, photo, and dollar bills on your altar or in your wallet/ purse. You can throw away the rice and corn.

OPEN ROADS TO OPPORTUNITY SPELL

Sometimes when we have a goal, there are unconscious beliefs that block us from easily achieving that goal or desire. These unconscious beliefs form because of various circumstances in life. It is important to remove any limitations that may keep you from the opportunities you are trying to create. This spell is designed to brush away any obstacles in the way of your success so that you can achieve your goals effortlessly. It will help you cleanse the energy surrounding you so you can be fully aligned with whatever you wish to manifest. If you feel stuck, this spell could also show you a new way forward and pave different paths to success.

In this spell, you will be literally washing away all the energy that is not serving you. Use this spell before you start something new, or even before performing another abundance spell. It is always good to clear the path to success so you can reach your goals more easily. Life is more fun when it feels like you are breezing through it. I do this spell all the time because I pick up new energy daily.

MAGICAL TOOLS

A bathtub, or a shower and a bucket

An herbal smoke wand, incense, or a high-vibrational spray

Two pieces of petition paper

A pen

Two orange candles

Open Roads anointing oil (or rosemary essential oil mixed with a carrier oil)

Two candleholders

Three pieces of fresh or dried mandarin

Dried or fresh mint

Dried or fresh rosemary

A lighter or matches

INSTRUCTIONS

Before beginning, decide whether you are going to take a bath or a shower as part of this spell.

1. Cleanse your space with incense, an herbal smoke wand, or a high-vibrational spray. Gather your magical tools.

2. On one piece of petition paper, write down what you are releasing. Describe what you think is blocking you, including any emotions, old energy, or obstacles that are standing in the way of your success. When you are finished writing, fold the paper once, away from your body.

3. On the second piece of petition paper, write down your intention. Write exactly what you want, and make sure to write as if it has already happened. Your intention may be something like "I am so happy and grateful that the roads are already open for success so that I can…" When you are finished writing your intention, fold the paper one time toward you. Then, set your petition papers to the side.

4. Pick up one of the unlit orange candles. Using the pen or another pointy object, inscribe the word *release* on the candle, writing from the wick toward the base of the candle.

Then, slather anointing oil on the candle in the same direction. While you are anointing the candle, state what you want to release. Place the candle in a candleholder.

5. Pick up the second unlit orange candle. Inscribe the word *attract* on the candle, writing from the base toward the wick of the candle. As with the first candle, cover it in anointing oil, but make sure to do so from base to wick. As you are anointing this candle, state what you want to call in and your intention for this spell. Then, set the candle in its holder.

6. Set the candleholders safely near the bathtub or shower. Carefully place the petition paper of what you want to release under the first candle, then place the petition paper of what you want to attract under candle two.

7. If you are going to take a bath, fill up the bathtub and make sure the temperature of the water is to your liking, but don't get in yet. If you are going to take a shower, fill up a bucket or container with warm water that you can have near you during this process. When your bath or bucket is filled, add three drops of anointing oil to the water.

8. Add three pieces of mandarin to the bath or bucket to call in prosperity and wealth. Add the mint to open up paths to new opportunities. Lastly, add the rosemary to clear any misunderstandings and to promote clarity.

9. When you are ready to step into the bath or shower, light the orange candles. Light the candle of release first, then the candle of attraction.

10. After the candles are lit, step into the shower with your bucket of water or get into the bathtub. Make sure to keep the candles in your line of sight the whole time so you can make sure they are burning safely, and never leave them unattended.

11. During your bath or shower, splash the beautiful road-opening water all over your physical and energetic body. Imagine yourself achieving your goal, and feel how happy, abundant, and free you are. You can also repeat your intention out loud.

12. When you feel that the spell is complete, say, "Thank you. It is done." You can stay in the tub or shower as long as you like after the spell is finished.

13. Let the candles burn out, making sure you do not leave them unattended. When the candles have extinguished themselves, your spell is done. You can then dispose of the wax, petition papers, mandarin pieces, and herbs in your trash can. As you go about your day, remain open to new ways of doing things, new opportunities, and the open roads that show up for you.

WEALTHY ME SPELL

This is a powerful spell that will call in more money, abundance, and prosperity in all areas of your life. If you want an upgrade in your life, this is the perfect spell for you. When you are performing this spell, remain open to all possibilities and ways for money and wealth to flow in. I once had a client set the intention of manifesting a million dollars in her bank account through her online business. She remained open to other ways money might flow in, and she was able to manifest a million dollars in less than a year. The funny thing was, the money didn't flow in through her business as she had intended. Instead, it came from another source of income that had not seemed plausible at the beginning of her manifestation process.

This spell will invite massive change into your life, so only perform this spell if you are truly ready to claim the abundance that is your birthright. Just like my client, be open to how the spell will bring you wealth, and expect miracles. This spell might bring instant abundance into your life, or it might not, because it is focused on creating long-term success. It is important to continue your other wealth witchery practices after this spell is cast so that you are in the frequency of attracting wealth. The Wealth Journal formula in chapter 8 complements this spell very well and will help you speed toward your results.

Before you start this spell, pull out your Wealth Journal and once again write down the qualities of the next-level, wealthy version of yourself. Write down the thoughts and beliefs you will have once you achieve this goal. Write down all of the things you will be doing and experiencing as the wealthy you. Once you have total clarity about all of this, begin the spell.

MAGICAL TOOLS

An herbal smoke wand, incense, or a high-vibrational spray

Nine crystals of your choice

Three gold or green birthday candles

Three candleholders or small plates

A lighter or matches

INSTRUCTIONS

1. Cleanse your space with incense, an herbal smoke wand, or a high-vibrational spray, then gather your magical tools.

2. Arrange the nine crystals in the shape of a big triangle. The triangle should be big enough for you to stand inside.

3. Place each candle in a holder, then place one at each of the three corners.

Crystal grid

4. While standing outside of the triangle, light the candles. As you light them, begin to see the flames and the crystals creating a powerful sacred space within the triangle.

5. Close your eyes and hold out your hands, palms facing the triangle. Imagine a golden light beaming out of your palms and into the triangle. Then, visualize the highest-level version of yourself inside of the triangle. Imagine the version of yourself that is filled with abundance and wealth. What do you look like? What do you dress like? How do you hold

yourself? How do you smell? What beliefs do you hold? How do you feel?

6. When you have fully envisioned the wealthy version of yourself and you are satisfied with it, open your eyes and step into the triangle. Become that very same version of yourself.

7. Feel a tingling golden light surrounding your energetic body, then moving into your physical body, illuminating every cell, muscle, and nerve.

8. Close your eyes once more. Imagine transporting yourself to the future. See the events playing out through the eyes of your future self. Instead of looking at the events as a third person, immerse yourself in your rich witch essence. Experience and feel yourself achieving all of your goals. Look at yourself deeply, and notice how you look, how you feel, and how you carry your body as you breathe in this space. When you feel ready, you can step out of the triangle, now embodying the wealthy version of yourself. Your spell will be complete once the candles burn out.

You can dispose of the candle wax in the trash or bury it in your yard. Then, collect your crystals and set them in special places such as by your bed, on your desk, or on your altar. Or, if you feel like you are finished with the crystals, you can cleanse them with herbal smoke or spray and reuse them in another spell.

Now that you have fully become the wealthy version of yourself and you know what it feels like to be that person, you can step into this version of yourself at any time of day. This spell's key to success is to make decisions as the wealthy version of yourself. Which choices would you make as this person? If you ask yourself that question before making a decision, big or small, you will manifest more wealth and abundance quicker than ever before.

RICH BUSINESS CHARM SPELL

All successful inventions and businesses start with an idea. The charm bag you will create in this spell is designed to help you receive an inspiring business idea that leads to abundance. You might have an idea for a massive project that will make you a lot of money, or you might come up with a smaller idea that could help you take the next step toward your goal of massive wealth. Whatever comes through will be the perfect idea for you to take action upon.

These ideas for riches might not show up the way you think they will. They also won't come with exact instructions that tell you what to do next. Stay focused on what you are manifesting and enjoy the journey you are being guided to. The more you work with your charm bag, the more you will connect to the energy of your business.

MAGICAL TOOLS

An herbal smoke wand, incense, or a high-vibrational spray

Petition paper

A pen

A green or gold charm bag, homemade or purchased

Dried mandarin peels

Dried basil

A cinnamon stick

Abundance crystals of your choice

Three coins

Something gold

Your Wealth Journal

INSTRUCTIONS

1. Cleanse your space with incense, an herbal smoke wand, or high-vibrational spray and gather your magical tools.

2. On the petition paper, write how you would feel if you already manifested the thing you most desire. What emotions would you be feeling if you were running the business of your dreams? Imagine exactly what your business would look like. Write down three things you feel at this very moment that you connect to that experience of success. When you are done, fold the paper once, toward you, and put it in the charm bag.

3. Start filling the charm bag with the dried mandarin peels, basil, cinnamon stick, and crystals you have chosen for this spell. Add the three coins and something gold as well. As you put each item into the bag, speak to the existence of one aspect of your business. For example, "I am grateful I have an amazing team that supports me in running my business successfully." Whatever you want your business to be like, speak it out loud.

4. When all the items are in the charm bag, hold the bag to your heart and say, "I now activate this magical charm to help me manifest a successful business that I love." Imagine a green light emitting from your heart space and connecting to the bag, infusing your charm with your intention.

5. Continue holding onto the charm, or at least have it touch you. Take out your Wealth Journal. Write "If I were running a successful, wealthy, and fun business, I would be…" Then, fill in the blank with whatever comes to your mind first. Don't second-guess your thoughts, just write them down. If they don't make sense, you can analyze what you are channeling later. What you are doing here is connecting to the energy of your business—what it most wants to be and how

it wants to show up in your world. When you are aligned to the frequency of your business, then the messages that appear will come from a place of you already accomplishing your goal. Your writing could be as short as half a page or as long as five pages or more; it is totally up to you.

6. After you are finished writing, look over what you wrote and make sense of it. How can you connect it to your everyday life? Come up with three actions that can get you closer to the business of your dreams. One of the actions I always include is to find a coach or a mentor. I look for someone who is already successful at what I want to do and can share the "cheat sheet" to success. After you write down three inspired actions, get out there and watch your business be birthed.

7. The more you work with your charm bag, the more potent your connection will be, and the more opportunities will arrive for you. You can keep your charm bag with you, on your desk, on your altar, or wherever feels best for you. It is best to talk to your charm bag or touch it daily. You can even sprinkle it with anointing oil or moon water to supercharge its magic.

FAME AND FORTUNE SPELL

When you are ready to be seen and heard, to inspire the world with your magic, and to live in abundance, then it is time to use this spell. This spell will not be for everyone, because not everyone wants to be famous or well-known. This spell is for those who are ready to step into the spotlight and share their wisdom with a larger audience. You will know when you are ready because you will have a deep yearning to inspire others. If you are ready to activate your radiance and stand out, then this spell was crafted specifically for you.

MAGICAL TOOLS

An herbal smoke wand, incense, or a high-vibrational spray

A photo of you

Photos of celebrities or influencers that inspire you

The Star tarot card

Gold or white string

A gold candle

A candleholder

A lighter or matches

Your Wealth Journal

A pen

INSTRUCTIONS

1. Cleanse your space with incense, an herbal smoke wand, or high-vibrational spray. Gather your magical tools.

2. Stack the photo of you, the photos of celebrities or influencers that inspire you, and the Star card together, then wrap them with string eight times. Each time you wrap the string around, binding the images, say, "I now activate my gifts of fame and fortune and star magic." Then, place the wrapped images under the candleholder.

3. Place a gold candle in the holder and light it. As you light the candle, say, "Famous and fortunate I shall be. Fame and fortune come to me." Repeat this three times and imagine a beautiful golden light surrounding you and the candle.

4. Next, grab your Wealth Journal. Write down what it feels like and looks like to have fame and fortune. Keep the lit

candle within your line of sight as you write. List everything that you want. Make sure to include positive intentions such as "I will be respected by my audience." Including positive intentions is important because you want to make sure that you gain notoriety through heart-centered actions and that your fame is for your highest good.

5. When the candle has burned itself out, that means your spell is complete. You can discard the candle wax in your trash can or bury it in your yard. Keep the wrapped images with you, preferably someplace you will see them every day, or leave them on your altar. Once you feel you have achieved the level of fame and fortune you want, or you have seen a movement in that direction and are satisfied, you can unbundle the images. Discard whatever is not needed and use herbal smoke or a spray to cleanse anything you want to reuse in future spells.

MILLIONAIRE MONEY SPELL

There is something so magical about the idea of being a millionaire. It is a dream I have for everyone reading this book. No matter where you are in life or how big your bank account is, if being a millionaire is something you desire, it is possible. What if you devoted 1 percent of your energy to becoming a millionaire every day? Think how much closer you would be to having $1,000,000 by the end of one year.

It's true, some people don't want to be millionaires; they would be quite happy to make a six-figure salary. But how fun would it be to say, "I am a millionaire"? This spell is to help you tap into the excitement and joy of becoming a millionaire. If you are offended by the concept of being a millionaire, or if you are desperate to be a millionaire, revisit the previous chapters to clear your money blocks and create a better relationship with money before attempting this spell.

MAGICAL TOOLS

An herbal smoke wand, incense, or a high-vibrational spray

Petition paper

A pen

An envelope (green or gold, if you'd like to add color magic)

Eight coins

INSTRUCTIONS

1. Cleanse your space with incense, an herbal smoke wand, or a high-vibrational spray. Gather your magical tools.

2. Think about why you want to be a millionaire and all of the things you could do with a million dollars. Make sure you have total clarity on this goal. Then, write the following statement on the petition paper: "I am so happy and grateful that I am now making millions of dollars easily. I accept this or something better. Thank you, and so it is." Fold the paper one time toward yourself, rotate it to the left, and fold it once more toward yourself.

3. Put the paper inside of the envelope, then add the eight coins. As you are putting them in, say, "One, two, three, and flow. Coins of abundance, multiply. Eight coins to millions, it will grow." Seal your envelope well.

4. Next, go outside and find a tree you feel connected to. Bury your envelope near the base of the trunk. Make sure to bury

it deep enough that no animal can dig it up. When you are done filling the hole back up, ask the tree to watch over your coins and help them grow into millions.

CLIENT ATTRACTION SPELL

Are you an entrepreneur, a CEO, or someone who makes more money when you have more clients? How would you like to be a client magnet and attract the right clients to your business? This is a spell to activate your client magnetism and expand your success container. It will allow you to connect your energy to your future clients'. Your clients will be able to connect to your energetic field before they meet you in the physical realm. If you have a certain type of client you would like to work with and are trying to call them in, then you need to vibrate at the same frequency and energy as they do. The Client Attraction Spell will help you raise your energetic vibes to match those of your ideal client so that they will magically appear in your life. Imagine waking up to an inbox full of people ready to work with you!

MAGICAL TOOLS

An herbal smoke wand, incense, or a high-vibrational spray

Two bowls

Twenty-two small items that inspire feelings of abundance; I like to use crystals (use red or pink items to magnify the attraction magic)

A yellow candle

A candleholder

Petition paper

A pen

Dried or fresh red rose petals

A lighter or matches

Your Wealth Journal

INSTRUCTIONS

1. Cleanse your space with incense, an herbal smoke wand, or a high-vibrational spray, and gather your magical tools.

2. Fill one bowl with the twenty-two items you chose. The number two represents partnership and relationships. When you add the numbers of twenty-two together, two plus two equals four, which represents the building of a sturdy foundation in tarot and numerology.

3. Place the second bowl, which should be empty, on the right-hand side of the first bowl.

4. Secure the candle in its holder and set it between the bowls. Make sure to leave enough room around the candle that it will not burn the bowls when lit.

5. On the petition paper, write down the kind of clients you would like to attract. Include the number of clients you would like to attract as well. Make sure to write these intentions as if they have already happened. For example: "I am so happy and grateful that I have a minimum of [number] clients who are…[qualities of the clients you want]. Thank you, and so it is." When you are done writing, fold the paper toward you once and put it in the empty bowl.

6. Next, spread the red rose petals in a circle around the two bowls. Do this with a smile, and imagine pink smoke emitting

from your heart and encircling the two bowls you are sprinkling the rose petals around. You are creating a safe, beautiful, powerful space for your clients to join you.

7. When you are ready to activate the spell, light your candle. As you do so, say, "I illuminate this candle to share my light and magic with my soulmate clients, and I call them in with ease, flow, and fun."

8. Staying near the candle, close your eyes and imagine a beautiful, open space. The space could be an office, a room full of expensive furniture, an open field, or even the beach. Whatever you visualize, this is the magical space you will be holding energetically for your clients. They will first encounter your energy before they meet you physically. Imagine your clients streaming into this space, maybe shaking your hand as they come in. Welcome them and enjoying sharing this space with them. See them loving the space you have created and having a really good time. Then, imagine your heart space lighting up with a pink glow and connecting to all of their hearts like a laser beam. When you are finished witnessing the connection, you can open your eyes.

9. Next, take the twenty-two items from the first bowl and individually place them in the second bowl, which was empty except for your petition paper. Each time you move an item over, say, "Thank you." You are now symbolizing your clients coming into your space in the physical realm.

10. If your candle is still burning, take time to journal about three actions you can take now to call in these clients. Perhaps you will make a social media post, reach out to past clients, or ask for a referral.

11. When the candle finishes burning, the spell is over. You can throw the wax and petition paper in the trash or bury them in your yard. Scatter the rose petals under a tree to give them back to the earth.

12. To amplify your spell, visualize the energetic space that holds your clients daily and connect with them on a heart-to-heart level each day. When you do this, you might visualize new clients showing up, or the clients in the space may become even more excited as real-life clients start to flow in. Taking aligned actions and reaching out to clients is also very important when it comes to this spell.

WINNING MONEY SPELL

I am a gambler and definitely love winning money. You could say that when I gamble, I'm really investing, because I don't put money down on something if I believe I can lose. Having this spell in your back pocket when you have a chance to win money calls in abundance and can help you get lucky. A big part of winning money is being super confident that you are already a winner. The most important tool in this spell is your unshakable belief that you are a winner. Be in that energy.

Disclaimer: Using this spell to win the lottery is possible, but you have to really believe it can happen for you. If you are trying to win millions of dollars but you only have $10,000 in your bank account, it'll be a long shot. It might take time and additional work to adapt to the energy of winning millions, so I cannot guarantee you will win big money all the time. It is important to know your money manifesting limits and beliefs, and it is even more important to do the work provided in this book. If you do, you will have a higher chance of calling in your desired abundance.

MAGICAL TOOLS

An herbal smoke wand, incense, or a high-vibrational spray

A green candle

A candleholder or plate

A lighter or matches

A tiger's eye crystal

The largest dollar bill you have

Gold, white, or green string

Anointing oil (optional)

Magical herbs (optional)

Gold glass glitter, which is friendlier for the environment than regular glitter (optional, but can supercharge your spell)

INSTRUCTIONS

1. Cleanse your space with incense, an herbal smoke wand, or a high-vibrational spray. Gather up your magical tools.

2. Pick up the candle. If you choose to, you can put abundance or luck anointing oil on the candle and then roll it in some magical herbs or glitter. Secure the candle in the candleholder or on a plate.

3. As you light the candle, say, "I am illuminating the path for my money wins now."

4. Next, pick up a tiger's eye crystal and hold it to the middle of your forehead. With the crystal near your third eye chakra, imagine yourself winning money. Envision whatever you

would need to see in order for you to believe that you have won. Is it the balance of your bank account, a big check, or perhaps you being declared a winner? Whatever gives you the most powerful charge is what you need to envision. Imagine it with all of your senses. See it happening, hear it happening, feel the emotions when you win, and maybe even smell or taste this new reality that you are creating.

5. When you are finished with your visualization, wrap everything up in a golden bubble and imagine the bubble leaving the top of your head and being sent into the Universe.

6. Next, take the tiger's eye crystal and wrap the dollar bill around it. Tie these objects together with string.

7. After the crystal and dollar bill have been wrapped tightly, hold the object in the palms of your hands and say, "I thank you, Universe, for gifting me the winnings of [amount you want to win] or more. And so it is."

8. Don't leave your candle unattended. When it has finished burning down, that is when the spell is complete. You can dispose of the wax in the trash can or bury it in your yard.

9. After completing the spell, the best place to keep your winning money talisman is in your pocket. If you have a jacket with pockets, keep it there when you are trying to win money. The next best place is in your pants pocket. If you do not have pockets on your clothing, you can place it in your bag. It is important to try to keep the talisman as close to your heart as possible. Carry this magical talisman until you have manifested winnings, or until you feel like you don't need it anymore.

SIMMER POT PROSPERITY SPELL

The Simmer Pot Prosperity Spell is fun and easy, and it makes your space smell divine. A simmer pot is created when you put herbs and spices in a pot of water, set it to simmer on the stove, and let the aroma fill the air, like potpourri but fresher. As the steam and aroma fill the air, so does the energy of what you are creating. A simmer pot will fill your space with positive intentions and high-vibrational frequencies. In doing this spell, you will be calling more prosperity into your life as you combine botanical correspondences with your intentions.

The main magical tool in this spell is the simmer pot. You can use any pot for this spell, but make sure it is a pot that you only use for spell work. Don't mix pots that you cook with and those you use for magic. You can also use a cauldron or Japanese *donabe* for this spell. I have a mini cast-iron cauldron wax warmer in my office that works amazingly well.

Caution: If you or anyone in your household are allergic to any of the ingredients listed, please do not use them. Your simmer pot is not meant to be ingested; do not consume.

MAGICAL TOOLS

An herbal smoke wand, incense, or a high-vibrational spray

A pot

Water (use charged moon water for extra magic)

A cinnamon stick

Mandarin slices, with or without the peel

Five-spice powder (a Chinese spice blend)

Eucalyptus, fresh or dried

Cloves, fresh or dried

Chamomile, fresh or dried

One bay leaf

A pen

INSTRUCTIONS

1. Cleanse your space with incense, an herbal smoke wand, or a high-vibrational spray and gather your magical tools.

2. Start by putting some water into your simmer pot. The less water there is, the more the fragrance will fill up the room. If you are sensitive to fragrances, use a lot of water; you do not need to be able to smell the simmer pot for the spell to work.

3. Place the pot of water on the stovetop. Heat the water to a boil, then turn it down to a low heat so that it begins to simmer.

4. While the water is simmering, add a cinnamon stick, a mandarin, some five-spice powder, and eucalyptus, cloves, and chamomile. Each time you add in an ingredient, say out loud, "Thank you, [ingredient], for bringing more prosperity into my life."

5. After all of the ingredients have been added to the pot, get out your bay leaf and pen. Write your intention on the bay leaf, or use key words and symbols to represent your intention. Make sure to write as if your intention has already come true. Then, hold the bay leaf to your heart space and speak your intention out loud before dropping it into the simmer pot. I like to use a wooden spoon to push the bay leaf down to make sure that it goes all the way to the bottom, past the other ingredients.

Simmer pot with spell ingredients

6. Activate your spell by stirring it clockwise three times. Say your intention aloud three more times.

7. Allow the water and magical ingredients to simmer as the mixture fills your space with amazing aromas and energies. You can let it simmer for as long as you desire; it could last several hours as long as you maintain the water level. Make sure to keep an eye on it. If you have to leave the house, you

can turn the stovetop off and reactivate the spell when you come back as long as the ingredients have not melted all the way down yet.

8. When you are finished, turn off the stovetop and let the ingredients cool. You can throw the ingredients away or dump them in your garden. After washing and cleansing your simmer pot, you can place it on your altar for other richuals and spells.

STEPPING THROUGH THE ABUNDANCE PORTAL SPELL

A portal is like a gateway to what you want. I love working with powerful energetic portals, such as on August 8, which is the Lion's Gate Portal. The Lion's Gate Portal is when the star Sirius aligns with the Sun in Leo. In Western astrology, the sign of Leo is often associated with lions. The number eight is associated with abundance, power, and infinity. Therefore, this gateway (8/8) has a special energetic significance.

This portal spell can be used anytime, but it will be amplified if you pair it with a magical astrological date like 8/8 or 11/11. The spell will open a magical path to your desired outcome and the result of your intentions. Portal spells can help collapse time to connect you to your goals more quickly. Instead of waiting five years for your goal to arrive, it may happen in two to three years. This portal spell is very powerful and may shift your reality instantly.

Before you perform this spell, make sure that you know exactly what you want and who you want to become. The more specific you are, the faster the Universe can bring you what you want. Make sure to add "This or something better" to your intention, and get ready to step into the reality that is for your highest and best good.

MAGICAL TOOLS

Incense or an herbal smoke wand

Petition paper

A pen

An ashtray or another fireproof dish

A lighter or matches

High-vibrational spray (optional)

INSTRUCTIONS

1. Cleanse your space with incense, an herbal smoke wand, or a high-vibrational spray. Gather your magical tools.

2. Write your intention on the petition paper, then fold it once toward you. Put your petition paper in the center of an open doorway. Then, place a fireproof dish on top of the petition paper.

3. Light incense or an herbal smoke wand and use the smoke to trace the shape of the door. Imagine a golden light surrounding the door. When you are finished, put the incense or smoke wand on top of the fireproof dish in the center of the doorway.

4. Hold your hands out and feel your energy connect to the energy of the golden doorway. Say, "I now open this abundance portal to my future reality."

5. When you feel like the golden light covers you and everything around you, imagine what it will be like to have manifested your intention. What does it look like, feel like, and sound like? Imagine the future version of yourself who has already achieved your goals.

6. Still holding on to the energy of your future self, step over the items in the doorway and into the portal that you have created. You are stepping into your future self.

7. As you stand on the other side, take a moment to connect to the feelings of your new reality and the new world you have just created.

8. Close the portal by picking up the incense or smoke wand and tracing the doorway again. Say, "The abundance portal is closed. The abundance portal is closed. The abundance portal is closed."

9. Keep the petition paper somewhere safe, such as next to your bed, in your Wealth Journal, or on your altar. Leave it there until you achieve your current goal or until you are switching focus to another one.

10. Here is a bonus wealth witchery tip: Note which scent the incense or smoke wand had. From this point forward, every time you use the same scent, you will be reminded of this spell and the highest-level version of yourself, and you will be able to tap into that frequency. Navigate your life in the present with the energy of your future self. The more you do this, the more you will accelerate the magic of the spell, so you will see results more quickly.

BLING-BLING SPELL

Would you like more bling-bling in your life? This spell is designed to manifest material items like Gucci loafers, a Chanel bag, a diamond engagement ring, your dream home, or that fancy car you've been eyeing forever. If you want nice things, rich witch, you can have them! When you desire something, it is meant for you, even if it is something that other people think is a waste of money.

I love buying designer bags and shoes, but I stopped for a few years because someone told me it was a waste of money. I listened to this person because they had more money than me, so I thought they knew better than me. But when I stopped buying what I wanted, my money flow became blocked because those things truly made me happy and helped me express who I am. When I let go of that other person's limiting belief and chose to believe I could be rich *and* have all the things I wanted, I started to triple my income.

If you want to be surrounded by luxury, you can be. This spell will call in all the bling-bling you desire! Please make sure you read through the spell in its entirety before beginning, as there are several ways to set up the spell depending on what you want to manifest.

MAGICAL TOOLS

An herbal smoke wand, incense, or a high-vibrational spray

A picture of yourself with your face showing clearly

Tape or glue

A blank piece of paper

A picture of the material object(s) you desire

A pen

INSTRUCTIONS

1. Cleanse your space with incense, an herbal smoke wand, or a high-vibrational spray and gather your magical tools.

2. Take a moment to close your eyes and focus on what you desire. Visualize yourself holding it, wearing it, driving it, or living in it. The most important part is to get in touch with how you feel when you have the thing you want most.

3. When you are done visualizing your reality, tape or glue the picture of yourself onto a blank piece of paper.

4. Cut out the picture of what you desire and put it on the same piece of paper that you put your picture on. Make sure the image of you want is touching the picture of you. If you are manifesting a bag, for example, place it near your shoulder or hand. If you are manifesting a car or house, you can put those pictures on the paper first and then place your picture on top to represent you inside the car or house. Use your imagination to connect the images of yourself and what you most desire.

5. Pick up a pen and begin to write in the blank spaces on the page. Write how you feel and who you are as this future version of yourself. Surround your image with positive affirmations by making sure every sentence begins with "I am" or "I have." For example: "I am always provided for, and I have everything that I need, want, or require."

6. To activate this spell, hold your hands over the paper and take three deep breaths. With each breath cycle, imagine a white light around the paper glowing brighter and brighter. When you are done with the three activation breaths, imagine yourself leaping out of the photo with whatever it is that you are manifesting. See yourself jumping into the sky, then up into the cosmos to connect to that future timeline.

7. When you have sent your desires into the quantum field, return to the present moment. Put the piece of paper somewhere you will see it daily. Whenever you see this magical artwork, you will be reminded that what you desire is on its way to you, and you will get closer and closer to that bling-bling.

Spells that help you accelerate your goals are a tool that most people don't have. Now that you have tapped into your magical spell-casting skills and tried your hand at a few of them, you should be able to start seeing progress. As you get closer to your goals, opportunities for even more forward movement will show up in your life. Spells are designed to support you in these efforts. But remember, spell work is not as simple as just lighting a candle and being gifted a million dollars. You must make sure to take aligned actions after you have completed the spell work, which is only one aspect of manifestation.

Keep practicing. Sometimes certain spells will work better than others because your energy is unique, so pay attention to that. You may discover that you connect with money more easily when using a certain herb or crystal; if so, use it in your future spells. With enough time and practice, you may even create your own spells for success. Play, stay curious, and experiment with different spells to determine which work best for you. Your magical practice won't be the same as everyone else's.

In the next chapter, you will learn richuals that can guide you on your magical path throughout the year.

TEN
RICHUALS
THROUGHOUT THE YEAR

Everyone performs some kind of ritual every day. You can think of rituals as habits, such as brushing your teeth every morning or drinking coffee. Other rituals may be performed weekly, monthly, or yearly. There are also different kinds of rituals, such as marriages, funerals, rites of passage, and magical ceremonies, that are done periodically.

In this chapter, I will be sharing several richuals with you. Richuals are rituals that promote abundance and prosperity. The richuals in this chapter are just the beginning for your wealth witchery practice. The ultimate goal is for you to develop your own richuals, ones that are meaningful for you and that represent shifts or changes in your life. Enjoy these richuals from my personal spell book. I hope they inspire you to include magic into your daily routine. And remember, the more you believe in a richual, the faster abundance will follow.

NEW MOON MONEY RICHUAL

When the moon is new, it shares the powerful energy of beginnings. The new moon is the perfect time to start a new venture or to brainstorm a new idea. Even people who don't know anything about moon magic seem to naturally start something new during this lunar phase. After all, the moon's energy can affect the tides of the ocean, and the human body is about 70 percent water—the magic of the moon will have an effect on us too!

In this richual, you will be honoring the new moon phase and planting the seeds of your intention for a potent manifestation. Since you are using the moon to amplify your intentions and magic, you will be focusing on more than one intention during this richual. In my experience, the power of the moon holds a lot of energy when you use it for manifestation, and it can charge up more than one intention if we desire. (We are multidimensional beings, so we can also manifest many things at once if we have enough energy to charge our manifestations.)

This richual is something I do every new moon, and I have seen amazing results.

MAGICAL TOOLS

An herbal smoke wand, incense, or a high-vibrational spray

Your Wealth Journal

A pen

A tarot deck

INSTRUCTIONS

You may want to perform this richual outside, underneath the stars. The new moon is completely dark, so you won't be able to see it, but it is there.

Start by clearing your space with incense, an herbal smoke wand, or a high-vibrational spray, then gather your magical tools. Grab additional magical tools if you feel called to include them in your richual, such as candles, incense, oils, or crystals.

1. Open this richual by honoring the moon. Greet her and ask her for a blessing during this lunar cycle so that your intentions come true on or before the next full moon. Do this by simply having a conversation with the moon as you are look up at the sky. Speak as if you are talking to a friend or family member.

2. Take out your Wealth Journal and write down ten intentions you want to manifest before the next full moon, which will be about two weeks after the new moon phase. You can write anything you want, big wishes or small wishes. Make sure to be very specific about what you desire. Rather than writing "I want to be rich," write something like "I have $50,000 in my bank account, and it feels amazing!"

3. After you are finished writing your ten intentions, read them all out loud. Speak them to the night sky if you can. If you cannot go outside, imagine your voice being carried to the moon and the cosmos.

4. Set down your journal and pick up a deck of tarot cards. (If you don't have tarot cards, you can download a tarot deck app on your phone for under $5.) You are going to do a reading under the new moon. This reading will show you what energy is surrounding you during this time and

how you can move forward with aligned action. Shuffle the deck while asking the first question, then draw one card and arrange it in the spread. Repeat for cards two through six.

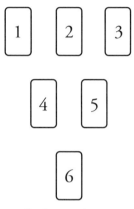

Card image layout

Card 1: What is the most important thing to focus on during this lunar cycle?

Card 2: How should I show up? Who do I need to be to reach my money goal?

Card 3: What am I not seeing that is blocking me from my money?

Card 4: What will support me in reaching my money with fun and ease?

Card 5: What magic is the new moon asking me to do right now?

Card 6: What is the aligned action I need to take to get me to my money goal?

5. When you finish pulling your cards, journal about any additional insights you receive from the card's artwork or the

deck's guidebook. If you want to take it a step further, you can also google the card and see what pops up as a message for you. Take your time and make connections that will help you get one step closer to your rich reality this lunar cycle.

6. After you are done journaling, you can either put away the cards or put them on your desk so that you are reminded of the actions you need to take and what's to come during the month. Next, copy your ten intentions onto a loose sheet of paper and place them somewhere you will see them daily so you stay connected to them, such as by your bed or on your altar. However, don't obsess over them. Trust that the Universe is making it all happen for you.

7. Revisit your journal every week, or every few days, to make sure you are on the path aligned with your money goals.

FULL MOON MONEY RICHUAL

The new moon and the full moon are the two lunar phases I consistently work with. For me, the new moon signifies the beginning of my manifestation cycle, and the full moon signifies the ending of the cycle. The previous richual was all about new moon magic, and in this richual, you get to close out and honor all you have learned during the two weeks between the new moon and the full moon.

When the full moon arrives, you will be able to see it visibly as it appears big, bright, and beautiful in the night sky. The energy during the full moon is very powerful, and you can harness the magic of the full moon to help you with your wealth witchery manifestations. During this lunar phase, the full moon's energy is all about letting go and releasing. This is not a time to start something new. However, you can finish what you've started, such as completing a project.

In this richual, you will be reflecting on creating a sacred space for new intentions to arrive during the next new moon. You will also be taking good care of yourself and your energy so that you have the capacity to receive abundance during the next new moon. Finally, you will be tapping into the energy of gratitude to amplify your magnetism.

MAGICAL TOOLS

An herbal smoke wand, incense, or a high-vibrational spray

A glass of water

A sticky note or a piece of paper and tape

A pen

Your Wealth Journal

Music (optional)

INSTRUCTIONS

If you can, set up your space outside under the stars. Pick a spot where the light of the full moon washes over you, or choose a spot where you can see the full moon clearly. If you are inside, sit by a window that lets in the moonlight.

1. Before you begin your richual, make sure you greet the moon and share how grateful you are for her, for the night sky, and for your life. Tell the moon what your intentions are for this full moon richual.

2. Start by cleansing your space with incense, an herbal smoke wand, or a high-vibrational spray. Gather your magical tools.

Add any other magical tools that you feel called to include in your ritual, such as candles, incense, oils, or crystals.

3. Set your glass of water in the moonlight so it can begin charging.

4. In this step, you are going to be moon bathing, which is basically placing yourself under the light of the full moon and soaking up all its light and magic. If you want to receive the maximum benefits of the magic of the full moon, go outside for this step. (If you can't go outside, then you can do this near a window or door where moonlight is flowing in.) Once you are under the moonlight, you can put on some music and/or move around under the moon, or you may feel called to just sit and meditate. Whatever you do will be perfect. The purpose of this step is to release anything that has been making you stressed, overwhelming you, or holding you back from reaching your goals.

5. When you are finished moon bathing, tune in to what you are grateful for. Say aloud what you are grateful for and why, or just think it in your head and send your thoughts to the moon. This is a very powerful tool for manifestation; it will charge your intentions with the beautiful magic of gratitude.

6. On a sticky note, write down the energy you would like to call in to help you manifest the intentions you have been focusing on. Think about the energy you will embody once you have what you want. You may choose words such as *courage*, *confidence*, *empowerment*, *beauty*, or *fulfillment*. Or maybe the energy you will embody is safety, since your goal is to have more money, and financial security makes you feel safe. You can also draw symbols on the sticky note, such as hearts, stars, or dollar signs, as long as they resonate with

you and have meaning. You may even want to include your rich witch symbol from chapter 7.

7. Next, attach your sticky note to your glass of water and hold the glass in your hands. Say, "I am ready and willing to call in [intention] right now. Thank you, mother moon, cosmos, guides, and ancestors for bringing me [intention]. I feel [what you wrote on your sticky note], and I know that I will be supported in everything that I want, need, and require. Thank you, thank you, thank you. And so it is."

8. Take a deep breath in, and then exhale into the water to lock in your magic.

9. With the glass of water still in your hands, stand up and start moving around. You can walk, sway, or dance—just be careful to not spill your water.

10. When you feel that the water has been infused with the energy of the moon and your magic, then drink it.

11. After you have finished drinking your water, take out your journal and write whatever comes to mind. You might have creative new ideas and come up with next steps immediately, or inspiration may strike in a day or two. See what comes up and do whatever feels right for you.

12. To close the richual, thank the moon for blessing you with amazing opportunities every day. Then, put away all of your magical tools, toss the sticky note, and expect miracles to flow in.

MERCURY RETROGRADE RICHUAL

I am sure you have seen articles and social media posts warning about Mercury retrograde. What does Mercury being in retrograde really mean? Simply put, retrograde means a planet appears to be traveling backward in its orbit from our position on Earth. This changes the influence of the planet. Mercury is the planet that rules communication and technology, so when it is in retrograde, you can expect these two areas of your life to be unpredictable. Don't get caught up in the idea of Mercury retrograde being a negative thing, though. I actually accelerate toward my goals during this time. It's all about your beliefs and knowledge. Understanding how to navigate this natural planetary energy makes all the difference.

This richual is designed to help you call in what you desire in record speed. Instead of manifesting your goal in three to five years, your intentions may manifest within one. Timelines speed up when you work with the powerful energy of Mercury, which allows your intentions to be communicated to the Universe at a faster frequency and flow into your life more easily.

Again, belief is everything! If you believe that Mercury retrograde is going to be a disaster because you keep reading posts about how bad it is, then it will be. If you believe that Mercury retrograde is going to fast-forward your manifestations and get you to your goals faster than you could ever imagine, then it will. Stop what you are doing right now and choose which belief you want to be responsible for. Affirm it and feel it in every cell of your body. If you chose to believe that Mercury retrograde is one of the best manifesting tools ever, then continue on with this richual.

As you can see, I do not follow the "normal" rules that many other witches and magical practitioners do. This Mercury retrograde richual is not about protection or being in survival mode because you are meant to thrive and be in abundance. That is what practicing wealth witchery means.

Before beginning your richual, you need to figure out when Mercury will be retrograde next. Timing is important in this richual; it should be activated before Mercury retrograde and before the shadow period. The shadow period of a retrograde planet occurs approximately two and a half weeks before the retrograde and after. The energy of the shadow period is less active and is viewed as a resting time, so to access the full power of Mercury, you will want to do this ritual before the shadow period begins. Do your research, and when you figure out when the next Mercury retrograde will occur, pick a date before the shadow period to perform this richual.

Now that you have the specifics locked in, spend some time thinking about the clear intention you are manifesting. You should be able to describe what you want in detail, as if it has already happened. I like to frame these intentions in gratitude statements. For example: "I am thankful for easily calling in $100,000 for my business in six months." If you manifesting a dollar amount, know exactly how much you desire and how you will use the money. If you need more guidance, you can revisit crafting an intention in chapter 5.

When you have set a date for your richual and have a solid intention that excites you and fills you with joy, then you are ready to gather your magical tools.

MAGICAL TOOLS

An herbal smoke wand, incense, or a high-vibrational spray

A blue candle

Open Roads anointing oil or coconut oil

Lavender, dried or fresh

A candleholder

A lighter or matches

A clear quartz crystal

A blank piece of paper

A blue pen

INSTRUCTIONS

1. Cleanse your space with incense, an herbal smoke wand, or a high-vibrational spray, and gather your magical tools.

2. Dress the blue candle with anointing oil by pouring a dime-sized drop of oil into your palm and smearing it on the candle with an upward stroke, from the base to the wick. As you are dressing your candle, say your intention in your mind.

3. Roll your candle in lavender. If you are using dried lavender, be mindful of the fact that your flame will be bigger while the candle is burning down, so make sure that you will be able to monitor your candle at all times.

4. Set the candle in its holder and then light your candle, stating your intention while doing so. Then, set a clear quartz crystal in front of your candle.

5. On a piece of paper, draw a big circle to represent the planet Mercury. Next, write your intention inside of the circle. Fold the paper once toward you.

6. Pick up the folded paper and hold it to the middle of your forehead, near the third eye chakra. Close your eyes and visualize the moment when your intention comes true. "See" it playing out in your mind. Really imagine it.

7. When you are done visualizing, spin three times to the right while still holding the paper to your third eye. Then, spin three times to the left in the same position. Jump up once, and as you land, imagine landing in the future that you were visualizing. Ground that into your reality now.

8. Remove the paper from your forehead. Place it underneath the crystal in front of your candle.

9. When the candle is finished burning, your richual is finished. Do not leave the candle unattended as it burns. If you need to leave, make sure you snuff the candle out, then repeat your intention when you relight the candle and resume the spell.

10. Throw away any leftover wax. You can keep the intention paper or throw it away—whatever feels best for you. Carry the crystal with you throughout Mercury retrograde and both of its shadow periods to ensure good fortune and to speed up your manifestation.

11. Your job now is to hold on to your visualization and be that version of yourself every day. Show up as if you have already achieved your goal, and make choices as that version of yourself. Always tap into the frequency of your rich witch self. Let go of "how" or "when" your intention is going to show up. Instead, allow yourself to be inspired by intuitive nudges to take action.

NEW YEAR'S RICHUAL

Even if you seek new beginnings and manifest new adventures daily, there is something extra magical about the celebration of a new year, right? No matter when you decide to celebrate the new year and the new you, this is the perfect richual. You can repeat this richual on several "new year" dates if you'd like. I typically perform this richual on the Witch's New Year, October 31; the New Year of the Gregorian calendar, which is January 1; on my birthday; and on Chinese New Year, which is calculated differently each year. I like to cover all my bases, just in case! Feel free to celebrate on multiple days like I do, or choose the New Year that resonates with you the most.

This richual is one of my favorites! I hope you love it as much as I do. Usually, the magical tools I use in spells and richuals are pretty simple, but since I only do this magic a few times a year, I splurge. Instead of writing on paper, I recommend writing on bay leaves, because they are one of the best tools to grant wishes. When you write on a bay leaf and then burn it, it will bring you abundant success and luck. A mandarin is also included because in Chinese culture, oranges (especially mandarins) bring amazing prosperity and are used in New Year's celebrations to call in good energy. The richual involves eating the fruit, so if you are allergic to mandarins or if you do not like them, choose another fruit that represents abundance to you.

Before you start the richual, come up with twelve intentions that you would like to manifest this year. These are what you will be writing on the bay leaves. Be specific and detailed about your goals, and remember to write them as if they have already happened.

MAGICAL TOOLS

An herbal smoke wand, incense, or a high-vibrational spray

Twelve bay leaves

A pen

An herb grinder or mortar and pestle

Cinnamon sticks or powder

Rosemary, dried or fresh

Basil, dried or fresh

Allspice powder

A white candle

Diluted lemon essential oil or coconut oil

A candleholder or fireproof plate

A lighter or matches

A mandarin

Fireproof dish or cauldron

Firesafe tongs or tweezers

INSTRUCTIONS

1. Cleanse your space with incense, an herbal smoke wand, or a high-vibrational spray, then gather your magical tools.

2. Write your twelve intentions on the bay leaves, one intention per leaf. Then, set the leaves aside as you prep your candle.

3. Use some sort of herb grinder or a mortar and pestle to grind the cinnamon, rosemary, basil, and allspice. Grind them as fine as you can and mix together.

4. Dress the white candle by pouring a dime-sized drop of oil into your palms. Dress the candle with an upward stroke, from the base to the wick. As you are dressing your candle, focus on feeling excited about how amazing this new year will be.

5. When your candle is covered in oil, roll it in the finely ground herbs. Make sure you cover the entire candle.

6. Set the candle in a candleholder or on a fireproof plate and light it. As you are lighting your candle, think of everything you will accomplish this year, including your twelve intentions. Think as if they have already happened.

7. Put the mandarin in front of the candle. This will infuse your fruit with the magic and energy of your intentions.

8. Set a fireproof dish or cauldron near the candle. Then, use the tongs or tweezers to pick up one bay leaf. Hold the leaf over the candle, and carefully light it on fire. Pass the bay leaf smoke around your mandarin, then gently set it on the fireproof dish or in the cauldron and let it burn out. Bay leaves burn quickly, and they can cause a big fire, so pay close attention and make sure you and your belongings stay safe. After the first leaf has burned out, pick up a second leaf. Repeat this process for all twelve bay leaves. Do not leave the candle or the leaves unattended while they are burning.

9. Let your candle burn itself out. When it has done so, grab your mandarin and eat it. This can help accelerate the speed with which your intentions become reality. When you are done eating the mandarin, bury the peel in your yard, or dry it and use it in a prosperity spell. Keep the bay leaf ashes on your abundance altar or bury them with your mandarin peels.

HONORING THE YEAR COMING TO AN END RICHUAL

Like all things in life, there are endings before new beginnings. To ensure you have space for the things you want to manifest in the upcoming year, you can perform this richual at the end of a year's cycle. As stated earlier, there are several days in a calendar year that may signify the end of a year for you. There is no set date for this richual. You can determine when the ending of the year is depending on which calendar and traditions you follow.

This richual will affirm all you have learned and the wisdom you have gathered over the past year, and it will help you let go of anything that is not needed moving forward. This richual is also to bless the upcoming year with good fortune. When you have completed another full year, it is time to ascend to the next level, and you won't be the same person anymore. Some of what served you before will no longer align with your new journey.

In this richual, you will first reflect on the past year and the adventures you had. Then, you will release negative emotions, beliefs, and blockages that are no longer serving you and that you no longer want. By purging what you no longer want, you will have created space for miracles in the upcoming year. After I do this richual, I often feel like a heavy weight has been lifted from my shoulders. I feel really light and free. I hope the same for you.

MAGICAL TOOLS

An herbal smoke wand, incense, or a high-vibrational spray

A piece of paper that you can rip apart

A pen

Your Wealth Journal

INSTRUCTIONS

1. Cleanse your space with incense, an herbal smoke wand, or a high-vibrational spray. Gather your magical tools. Feel free

to incorporate crystals, candles, anointing oils, or incense if you would like.

2. Sit for a few moments and reflect on your year. Close your eyes if you have to. What were the main patterns that showed up for you? What were the main lessons learned? How was this year different from the year before? How can you make it better next year? What did you love about the past year? What did you not love?

3. When you are ready, take out a piece of paper and write down everything that you want to release, some of which may have come up during your reflection. Include any emotions felt this year that you want to release, people you want to forgive and let go, places or things you are ready to release, doubts or fears that no longer serve you, and anything else you are ready to move on from. Write until your mind is blank and the list feels complete.

4. Then, fold the paper in half, facing away from you. Rotate it to the left and fold it in half again, facing away from you. Repeat this step until the folded paper is the size of your palm.

5. Hold the paper to your heart space and imagine that you are infusing the paper with pink light with every breath that you take. As you breathe in, the pink light gets brighter and brighter. Breathe in and out at least three times.

6. When you are ready and the paper is as bright as it can be, offer all of the things you wrote to the Universe to be let go. You can create your own closing prayer or say, "Dear cosmos, I offer you these emotions, thoughts, beliefs, people, places, and things that are no longer aligned with me. I am sending them to you with love. Please bless me with new

miracles and abundance in the coming year. Thank you, thank you, thank you. And so it is."

7. After you have said your prayer, rip up the paper and throw it away.

8. Next, get your journal and write down 111 things you are manifesting in the next year. Write as if these things have already happened by using the phrases "I have" and "I am." You can write anything you want; small and large intentions are both amazing.

9. When you are finished writing your 111 list, place it some-where you will see it every day, and expect miracles to come to you in the new year.

MONDAY MONEY RICHUAL

This is one of the most powerful money richuals I have incorpo-rated into my life. It is also one of the richuals my clients and I were most resistant to because it makes you look at your money! If you feel resistant to this richual and absolutely do not want to do it, read through the entire richual. If you still don't think the richual is needed after you have read through it, then I invite you to try it out for at least a month. The reason being, when we are the most resistant, this often indicates we are on the edge of a breakthrough, and the miracles and abundance we most desire are right around the corner—that is, of course, if we take the aligned actions we are resistant to.

If you don't change what you do in your life, then life will stay the same. Your life will change when you allow yourself to be uncomfort-able and push yourself out of your comfort zone. You never know, this could turn out to be one of your favorite richuals! Promise yourself that you will spend time with your money every Monday. If you absolutely cannot do this richual on Mondays because it is your busiest day of the week, then move it to another day. You could incorporate the Monday Money Richual into your life by doing it during a money date, if that resonates. The actual day that you perform this richual is not set in stone; you can choose when you want to do this practice as long as you do it once a week.

The Monday Money Richual is very simple and effective. The hardest part is actually doing it on a consistent basis. If you put in the effort and schedule it on your calendar, you will love how money responds to you. My clients and I have manifested tens of thousands of dollars by implementing what you are about to learn. This richual catapulted my business from making $2,000 per month to $30,000 revenue months, and all it required was five to fifteen minutes of my time each week!

MAGICAL TOOLS

An herbal smoke wand, incense, or a high-vibrational spray

Money anointing oil or diluted orange essential oil

A green candle (use a large pillar candle and relight it every week, or use a chime spell candle if you would like a new candle each week)

A candleholder

A lighter or matches

Your wallet

Dollar bills, any amount

A pen

A money tracker sheet or app

INSTRUCTIONS

1. Cleanse your space with incense, an herbal smoke wand, or a high-vibrational spray. Gather your magical tools.

2. Anoint your feet and/or your candle with money anointing oil. While you are putting on the anointing oil, repeat your intention in your mind repeatedly. Your intention should be the amount of money you'd like to manifest.

3. Place the green candle in its holder and light it. As you light the candle, repeat your intention.

4. Take out your wallet and feed it some money by placing physical bills inside. Make sure you tell your wallet how much you gave it, and really feel the joy of putting more money inside your wallet.

5. While you are feeling really blessed financially, this is the time to pay some of your bills, or to take care of anything that has to do with money. Here is a rich witch secret when it comes to paying bills: You want to feel good while doing it. If you send out negative vibes connected to money, then money won't want to come to you. When you look at your bills, think of how lucky you are to have the services or items you are paying for, or remind yourself that the lenders trust you so much. Think of how lucky you are to have been able to buy the things you bought or experience the amazing moments connected to the bill you are paying. As you pay the bill, love the money you are paying with, and set the intention that whatever you send out will come back ten times as much. A big part of this practice is showing love to your money and creating a safe space for it so that more money will want to flow in.

6. Next, look at your bank account(s) and send some sparkles and love. Look at the balance(s) and send the numbers love, no matter how much money you have. Tell the money in your bank account(s), "Thank you so much for being here, and more money is coming in!" Visualize your bank account balance growing to the number you desire.

7. Money Monday's main theme is to focus on your money in an uplifting way. The more energy you give to something, that is what will manifest in your life. A part of this, therefore, is to track your money. Track every single penny you have spent or earned this week on a physical or digital money tracker or on an app. It might be easier if you track your money every day and just add it up weekly—whatever works for you. As you track your money, you might realize how abundant you really are, and you may also become aware of where your money is leaking so you can plug up that hole. Don't overthink this step; just write down how much money came in and how much money went out.

8. Allow the candle to burn itself out. If you have to leave the room, snuff (don't blow) out your candle. When you relight it, state your intention again. This will keep your intention and the magic alive. After the candle has finished burning, cleanse the candleholder and throw away the wax.

You can add anything else you want to this richual. Maybe this is a time to meet with your abundance guides or do a spell for money flow. Your money days do not have to be completely the same; they can change week to week if you desire. Just be sure to include the main steps provided here to really connect with your money, track it, and help it grow. Make focusing on your money a pleasant experience. Don't ignore money or fear money. If you have been doing so previously, that's okay. Now is the time to change.

BIRTHDAY WISH RICHUAL

You probably already know when to perform this richual: your birthday! I believe there is some truth behind all legends, fairy tales, and superstitions, including the one about making birthday wishes. I believe making a wish on your birthday is a form of magic. This Birthday Wish Richual can add a powerful boost of magic to the wish you make while blowing out your candles. This is also an amazing present to give to someone if you want them to have an abundant year.

MAGICAL TOOLS

An herbal smoke wand, incense, or a high-vibrational spray

Petition paper

A pen

A small glass jar with cork or lid

One bay leaf

Three cloves

Three allspice berries

A cinnamon stick or ground cinnamon

A green or gold birthday candle

A lighter or matches

Your Wealth Journal (optional)

Birthday wish jar

INSTRUCTIONS

1. Cleanse your space with incense, an herbal smoke wand, or a high-vibrational spray and gather your magical tools.

2. On the petition paper, write ten wishes that you want to come true before next year's birthday. Date the bottom of your petition paper when you have finished writing your ten wishes. On the other side of the paper, write your full legal name.

3. Roll up the petition paper and put it in the glass jar.

4. On the bay leaf, write one word that represents the energy that you want to embody in the year ahead, then put that into the jar as well.

5. Add the cloves, allspice, and cinnamon to the jar.

6. Close the jar and set it on a flat surface, away from anything that is flammable. Pick up a birthday candle and heat the base of the candle with a flame until it begins to melt. Then, secure the birthday candle on top of the lid by firmly pressing the melting base onto the lid until the wax has set.

7. When the candle is secured, light the wick and say, "Today is my birthday, and what I desire will come true this year for my highest and best good. Thank you, thank you, thank you. And so it is."

8. Let your candle burn itself out. Remain nearby to make sure it burns safely. While you are waiting for your candle to burn down, you could journal about how magical this next year of your life will be.

9. The richual is finished when your birthday candle has burned out. Put your birthday wish jar by your bed or on your altar for a year of good luck and wishes manifested. Happy birthday!

DRESSING FOR SUCCESS RICHUAL

In the beginning of this book, I talked about how changing your identity (how you currently express yourself) is the one of the quickest ways to create change in your life. Once you have done the inner work, then you can focus on matching your external environment to what you have created internally. This richual is to help you ground all the magic you have done in the energetic realm and the mental realm. Your intentions need to be brought into the physical realm, because this is where you experience everyday life.

With this richual, you are going to infuse your clothing or accessories with magic so that when you put on those pieces of clothing, you will automatically embody that magical energy. This is a richual you can do every single day to ensure you have an amazing day and that you show up as your best self. This richual is especially useful if you have an important event coming up.

MAGICAL TOOLS

Clothes and accessories

An herbal smoke wand or a high-vibrational spray

INSTRUCTIONS

1. First, set an intention for who you want to be and what energy you would like to embody for the day. Maybe you want to feel more abundant, confident, or beautiful. Decide on a word or sentence that will help you have a joyful, successful day.

2. When you feel the energy you are claiming for the day, close your eyes and ask yourself, *Which color will create abundance for me today?* You will receive an answer immediately. It may come through as a thought, a word, or a visual of the color itself. You can hear it, see it, or even feel it. Allow whatever pops into your head first to be your answer. It's okay if you don't love the color or are surprised. Know that the message you received was from the Universe, and if you choose to wear the color provided to you, it will help you embody the energy you desire.

3. Next, browse your closet and choose clothing and/or accessories in the color you were guided to wear. Wear that color in whatever way possible; even if only a small bead on a necklace has that color, it is still magical.

4. When you have chosen what you are wearing for the day, cleanse the energy of your clothing with an herbal smoke wand or spray. Then, as you are putting on your clothing, affirm what you want to happen that day. I like to also say my intentions and some affirmations as I get dressed to make it more powerful. For example: "Because I am wearing my pink socks today, I will feel supported and loved while I call in more abundance." As you say your intentions and affirmations, make sure that you are feeling the emotions and energetic charges of them as well.

5. When you have finished getting dressed, smooth out your clothing and give yourself a few pats. Say, "And so it is." Now you are ready for the amazing, abundant day ahead!

LUCKY MONEY SHOWER RICHUAL

When I created this richual, all I could think about was how cool it would be if money just rained down upon me. It would be so fun to stand under a waterfall of money, right? This started out as a beautiful bath richual, but I had to stay true to who I am, and since I prefer to take showers, I created the Lucky Money Shower Richual. It has not let me down yet!

I like to perform this richual every day. It is very easy to do, and since showers are a part of my everyday life, I thought, *Why not create something magical that can amplify my wealth while I shower?* If performing this richual every day is too much for you, try to incorporate it every week or even on the first of the month. After your first Lucky Money Shower Richual, I hope you feel like a million bucks and want to do it as much as you can.

This richual might be the easiest of all of the richuals in this book. You don't need any magical tools, although you can add candles, herbs, or oils to enhance the experience and amplify the abundance magic if you wish.

MAGICAL TOOLS
None

INSTRUCTIONS
Note: I use the term "body section" in this richual. I consider the body section to be everything except your face and your feet.

1. Before you start the shower, ask yourself, *Which area of my life is blocking me from reaching my abundance?* When you have figured out an answer, then ask yourself, *Where am I holding that in my body?* Notice what comes up for you, as it is coming to your attention to be released. You may intuitively know the answer is in your chest, fingers, ears, or several areas of your body. Pay close attention to those areas during the next step of this richual.

2. Step into the shower. As you wash your hair (optional), your face, your body section, and your feet, repeat the following incantations:

   (If you are washing your hair that day) *As I cleanse my hair, I let prosperity flow through me.*

   As I cleanse my face, I let my beauty shine and attract divine money.

As I cleanse my body, I release any limita-
tions and activate my abundance.

As I cleanse my feet, I ground into mas-
sive wealth and luck.

After you have finished washing your feet, stand under the water and say:

I let go of what is no longer needed,
and I call back all my power.

I am lucky and rich. It is done, it is done, it is done.

Thank you, thank you, thank you.

If you feel called to make up your own magical phrases to include in this richual, then please do so.

3. When you are done showering, reenter the world knowing that you are blessed with luck.

GREEN SALT CRAFTING RICHUAL

This richual will teach you how to create green salt. Green salt can be used in any kind of money magic, including in spells, mojo bags, money jars, and so much more.

MAGICAL TOOLS

An herbal smoke wand, incense, or a high-vibrational spray

A mortar and pestle

Dried mint

Dried rosemary

Dried basil

Dried bay leaves

A large bowl

Moringa and/or matcha powder (I like to use mostly moringa and a dash of matcha, since matcha is a bit more expensive)

A spell spoon (spoon not used for eating or cooking—only for magic)

Salt (sea salt, green tea salt, table salt, or another kind of salt you have access to)

A jar or container

INSTRUCTIONS

While this spell can be performed any time—especially if you have run out of green salt and want more—choosing a day that is connected to abundance is recommended. The new moon or full moon phases are always a good time to create green salt, especially if the lunar phase lands on a Thursday or Friday, which will infuse your salt with extra prosperity energy.

As you are performing this richual, make sure your mind is focused on your abundance, the money you want, or your intention. Send good money vibes into your green salt as you are creating it. It helps if you smile the entire time!

1. Cleanse your space with incense, an herbal smoke wand, or a high-vibrational spray and gather your magical tools.
2. In a mortar and pestle, grind the dried mint. Do the same with the rosemary, basil, and bay leaf. Once all the herbs are ground, mix them together.

Green salt preparation

3. Pour the herbs into a large bowl. Then, pour an equal amount of moringa or matcha powder into the bowl. Using your stirring spell spoon, stir the mixture clockwise three times.

4. Do the same with the salt, adding an amount equal to the powder. Pour it into the bowl and stir it clockwise three times.

5. After you have finished stirring, hold your hands over the mixture. Give your green salt a purpose by saying an intention out loud. What do you want the salt to do for you? Do you want it to bring you more money, opportunities, or

abundance? Imagine a soft green smoke wafting from your hands and into the salt as you speak your intention.

6. Bottle up the green salt and keep it by your herbs or on your abundance altar until you are ready to use it.

Here are some magical wealth witchery ideas for using your green salt.

- Sprinkle green salt around your incense or candle holders. If you place incense or candles in a dish, you can use the green salt as a filler substance.
- Line doorways and windows to bring in abundant opportunities.
- Dress your candles with green salt to amplify money and abundance.
- Perform the following Green Salt Money Spell.

GREEN SALT MONEY SPELL

This is a quick and powerful spell that you can do with your green salt.

MAGICAL TOOLS

A firesafe plate

Green salt

Anointing oils

Nonflammable items that represent prosperity

A lighter or matches

INSTRUCTIONS

1. Set an intention for how much money you want to manifest in a month or a year. For example: "I am grateful to have made $10,000 each month easily and consistently" or "I have $50,000 in my bank account, and it keeps growing every month."

2. Use your green salt to draw a circle, clockwise, on a firesafe plate.

3. Drop your favorite anointing oils on the circle of salt, using one drop in each direction of the salt circle (north, east, south, and west). Don't drop too much oil, because it is flammable.

4. Decorate the inside of the circle with crystals, gold objects, herbs, coins, and anything that you relate to prosperity. Do not use dollar bills, as they are flammable.

5. When you are finished decorating, light the salt on one end. After you light your salt, say your intention for more money and visualize it being infused into the middle of the circle. As the flames dance, visualize them sending your intention to the Universe. Make sure you are practicing safe fire magic by watching the flames the entire time they are lit.

6. The fire will go around the entire circle. When the entire circle has burned out by itself, your spell is complete.

PROSPERITY FROG RICHUAL

I discovered this richual during a powerful meditation while writing my second book, *The Mandarin Tree: Manifest Joy, Luck, and Magic with Two Asian American Mystics*. This richual is a kind of abundance magic, as frogs represent good luck in many Asian countries. In Japan, for example, there is a superstition that if you have a frog on your coin purse or wallet, then money will consistently flow in. This richual is a similar concept: You will be using the magic of the prosperity frog to bring good fortune and wealth into your home.

MAGICAL TOOLS

An herbal smoke wand, incense, or a high-vibrational spray

Coins

Golden prosperity frog (found online or in a metaphysical shop)

A coin for the prosperity frog's mouth (optional; these usually come with coins, but if not, make sure the coin you use fits in the frog's mouth)

INSTRUCTIONS

1. Gather your magical tools and stand by your front door. Choose a flat surface where your prosperity frog will not be bothered or moved. Then, cleanse the space with incense, an herbal smoke wand, or a high-vibrational spray.

2. Lay coins on the flat surface. Prosperity frogs like to be elevated, so after placing the coins, set the frog on top of them. If your prosperity frog does not have a coin in its mouth, place one there.

3. In the mornings, turn the prosperity frog away from your home so that it faces outward. This way, the frog can go out and bring in money for you. When I turn my prosperity frog, I like to tell it what I want and ask it to go get it for me. Therefore, be intentional when turning your frog.

4. At night, turn the prosperity frog around so that it faces into your home. Thank your prosperity frog for all the money it has brought into your life. Now, it will guard and grow the money you have.

5. Repeat daily.

As you can see, the Prosperity Frog Richual requires two actions every day. These are very easy to do, but they are also very easy to forget about. I suggest setting two alarms so that you are reminded to complete your Prosperity Frog Richual. If you have a daily routine that requires you to leave the house, you could also turn the frog when you leave, then turn it again when you come home.

MORNING QUANTUM PORTAL RICHUAL

I think of a quantum portal as a gateway to the infinite possibilities of the quantum field. The quantum field is like a warehouse that holds everything you need and more. Whether or not you are aware of it, you access the quantum field through your aura (the energetic field that surrounds your body) and communicate with it daily through your energy and thoughts. Whatever you are thinking and feeling is being emitted into the quantum field and brought back into your reality. This richual will allow you to be intentional about what you send into the quantum field and, therefore, what you are manifesting into your life.

If you are already doing your wealth journaling, then this practice will amplify the intentions you have set for yourself. In this richual, instead of using written magic, you will be using your throat chakra and your voice to craft the best life ever. Your words are like spells that weave magic into your life and create what you are experiencing. You will be using the power of your voice to open the quantum portal and receive access to what you want.

This richual works best through repetition, which means you should do it every day if possible. It only takes a few minutes in the morning, and it will empower you to take aligned action during the day. The energy you tap into during this time will determine the energy of the rest of your day. This is a powerful manifestation tool, so I hope you love it.

MAGICAL TOOLS
Your Wealth Journal

A pen

INSTRUCTIONS
Find a quantum portal partner for this richual. Make sure to choose someone who is magical, fun, and excited to do this. This person could be anyone as long as they have the right mindset. I do this with a friend I met online and totally vibed with. She has the same energetic frequency as me, loves to dream big, and creates shifts in her life quickly. It is also super powerful to do this richual with your partner, because then you are both amplifying the life you desire. If you are unsure who to work with, know that you can do this richual with more than one person if you would like.

In this richual, you will be sending voice messages to each other. If necessary, you could use voice-to-text to send each other messages instead. If you and your quantum portal partner see each other every day, then I recommend speaking in person. Speaking out loud is a powerful part of this richual.

1. Start off by telling the cosmos that you are here and ready to step into the quantum portal. Say, "Dear cosmos, I, [name], am stepping into the quantum portal now."

2. Next, begin to record a voice memo or use voice-to-text to share what you are grateful for. (If you can talk to your quantum portal partner in person, do that instead.) Speak for forty-five seconds to a minute. Make sure to include *why* you are grateful for the things you are sharing. For example: "I am grateful for my chickens because they make me feel so happy, and they love to keep me company and cuddle with me." While you are speaking, feel the energy of gratitude. Then, send the voice memo or text to your quantum portal partner.

3. Share what you wrote in your Wealth Journal. Start off by writing, "It is [future date], and I am so happy and grateful that I have [whatever you want to manifest]." The phrases "I have" and "I am" will help you write as if it has already happened. This should take the bulk of your time.

4. After you are finished with step three, share what happened during the current day. Speak as if it has already happened. This will help your brain focus and call in what you want to achieve during the day and also attune you to good vibes. You could say something like, "Wow, today was so amazing. I had so many incredible things happen. I got/have/am/received…" Say as much as you want.

5. Lastly, lock in what you have just shared. I like to say "Thank you, thank you, thank you. And so it is. Manifest, manifest, manifest. *Pew, pew, pew!*" to my partner or out loud to myself. The last sentence is the sound of my manifestations being shot into the air, which always puts me in a good mood.

6. Once you are done with your portion of the richual, listen to what your partner has shared. Offer them supportive responses. Hype each other up and get into the frequency of excitement and joy. When you cheer each other on, you rise together. Remember to congratulate them as if what they want has already happened. For example: "Congratulations on manifesting that publishing contract today!"

11:11 RICHUAL

Do you see the numbers 11:11 or 111 everywhere? If not, maybe you will start noticing these numbers more often after reading this richual. This richual is designed to anchor you in the frequency of prosperity that these numbers share.

MAGICAL TOOLS

None

INSTRUCTIONS

This is one of my favorite richuals because it doesn't require any magical tools, and you can share the magic with your friends.

1. The 11:11 Richual is very simple. Basically, whenever you see the numbers 11:11 on the clock, or whenever you see

the number 111, stop and acknowledge that you are on the right path. These numbers are the Universe sending you confirmation that you are taking aligned action, and everything is going to work out.

Clock showing 11:11

2. Try to remember what you were saying or thinking about right before you saw this magical number, as the confirmation could be directly related to what you were focused on at that time.

3. While I'm in this magical energy, I like to make a wish and set an intention.

4. When you expect to be blessed or experience a miracle, it will happen. If you believe you are lucky, then you will be lucky. You create your own magic in life, so this 11:11 Richual is designed to remind you to be grateful for where you are so that you can call in more abundance.

These richuals are meant to support you on your manifestation journey. Being a rich witch is not a get-rich-quick scheme; it's something you already are, and it is a lifelong journey. These practices will ground you in your reality and allow your manifestations to show up more quickly. When you are intentional about the life you are creating rather than leaving it up to chance, you are far more likely to get what you want.

After doing these richuals, you might discover even more practices that align you with your goals. You might create them yourself, or you might come across them in another book. However you find other richuals, if you feel called to do them and they make you feel joyful and excited, then go for it! You can never do too much magic or dream too big. The more wealth you call in to every area of your life, the greater impact you can have.

ELEVEN
WHAT'S NEXT?

On your journey throughout this book, you have learned a lot about how to use magic to manifest more money, wealth, and abundance. I encourage you to put these magical exercises, spells, and richuals into practice in your life. Go slow. Perhaps you can start by being consistent with a few of the richuals in chapter 10 or by implementing daily spells one at a time. If you are someone who moves at a fast speed, like I do, perform a couple spells and at least one richual each month to move more quickly.

Success runs on momentum. When you are comfortable implementing richuals and spells, keep up the momentum. Don't stop once you have built up energy! I totally understand that life can get in the way, and you might get busy. However, the secret to never-ending money and opportunity is to have a consistent wealth witchery practice that is a priority, no matter what. This may mean you have to actually schedule time for your practice in your calendar. If my wealth witchery practice was not on my schedule, I would probably spend that time doing other things and not have time for my magic either—but then I wouldn't be living my best life right now! Your practice is all about being aware of what you are choosing for yourself. How much do you want the things you are intending to create in your life?

After you have done the spells, richuals, and magical exercises in this book, you might be wondering, *What happens next? When will my abundance manifest?* If you are wondering how to manifest more money and when it will come, then that is a great indicator that you should return to some of the previous chapters, such as chapters 5, 7, and 8. Revisit your money beliefs and blockages. Being anxious about whether or not your money is here yet is like saying that your money is not here. Instead of being in the energy of lack, simply focus on what you want and the feeling of already having that. Trust that the Universe has your back and is creating the most beautiful reality for you.

Sometimes things shift quickly. You could see results instantly, or it could take a few months or even years—you never know. Regardless, there will be signs along the way that let you know you are on the right track. It is important to be aware of these signs, because they can help you stay high-vibe and in the energy of manifestation. Signs can also help you maintain your belief that everything is in the process of happening for you. You might notice signs from your guides, angels, or the Universe. In fact, you may have seen these signs already! Your guides, angels, and the Universe can communicate through sentences or words that you read or through angel numbers like 11:11, 222, 333, 444, and so on. You might also get messages from a song if you hear lyrics that are exactly what you needed to hear in that moment. Messages can even come from the people around you. For example, if you are walking and all of a sudden, someone passing by says a phrase that answers the question you have, that may be a message for you. The Universe communicates with us in all sorts of ways! Stay connected to your inner guidance and pay attention to signs that you are on the right track to your abundance.

Soon after getting signs and confirmations, you might start to see more changes in the physical realm. Miracles might start to show up in your life, moving you closer to your goal. Let's say you are manifesting a promotion for yourself. You might get called to the office because they are letting you know you are being considered for a new position. Movement toward your goals—small or large—tends to happen during this time. You will notice that you are getting closer and closer to your goals.

Remember, once you have cast a spell or completed a richual, you have to follow the magic and go with the flow, wherever it takes you. If you are receiving random messages and signs telling you to do something that doesn't make sense, you should still give them a try. A client of mine received a message to sing in the car on her way to the mall if she wanted money to come in. Even though it wasn't something she normally did, she listened to the message, and she manifested $5,000 from a new client!

A lot of times, forward movement and opportunities come with challenges. In my experience as an entrepreneur, opportunity and abundance often come after I invest in a coach or mentor who can help me get to the next income level. Finding a coach is one way I take aligned action. Say I'm manifesting $30,000 revenue months for my business, and I cast a spell. The Universe might bring me $30,000 from new clients over time, but I will reach my goal faster if I take aligned action. Perhaps I first invest $10,000 in a coach who teaches me a new technique and *then* receive $30,000. Even my clients who work at salaried jobs have been able to create powerful changes in their lives by taking action. They pushed themselves out of their comfort zones and set higher sales and bonus goals; they applied for promotions that seemed out of reach and got them; they talked to their bosses about getting a raise.

The best way to know if you are on the right track is to check in with your heart, not your head. Ask your heart if what you want to do lights you up. Do you desire this? Will it make you happy, even if you are scared or doubtful right now? If it brings you joy and you are excited about it, then go for it! Don't let your subconscious mind and ego keep you where you are. As I shared in chapter 7, sometimes an idea or action is a good one, but we are resistant to it. That is why it is important to go through all the exercises in this book; they will make sure you have the clarity you need to know if something is or is not the right step for you.

Another sign that you are close to your goals is if you notice people around you getting the things you want. That means you are calling it closer and closer to your reality. Everyone is different, and you may have unique signs and feelings that indicate you are getting close to manifesting your goals. Personally, I notice these sorts of things happening when I'm really close to my goals: I start coughing, seemingly for no reason. My stomach might turn during my magical practices. When I'm chanting or speaking, I will start to yawn or tear up; sometimes this makes me very tired. Another sign is that I feel the need to clean, because I never enjoy cleaning! My hair may even part a different way all of a sudden. (Interestingly, students in my manifestation program noticed their hair changing when they were close to manifestation too.) While some of these signs are unpleasant, like my stomach turning, they make me happy because I know I'm shifting. Whatever signs and feelings happen for you, make sure you celebrate them and affirm that they are happening, even if you don't love them, because this means you are almost to your goal!

Another important part of this work is to address why your manifestations may not be coming true, as I mentioned previously. This is a loaded question, because we never truly know the reason why—there are so many variables! But I will do my best to remind you of some of the possibilities. If you are new to wealth witchery or manifestation, especially manifesting money, then you might still be building up your money muscles. The more you practice, the quicker your manifestations will arrive, and the stronger your inner magic will magnetize what you desire. If you are still not able to manifest what you want after lots of practice, then there may be something missing in your manifestation process. Maybe you are still in the process of figuring out what works best for you. If that is the case, keep implementing the tools in this book, follow the guidance provided to you, and continue to trust the process. Most importantly, *keep going*. You don't want to be the witch who stops three feet from gold and then turns around, right? Trust you are on the right path and keep at it. If someone offers you an opportunity, research it to see if it's right for you, and if everything checks out, say yes. If you come across a program that could teach you more about what you are trying to accomplish, then invest in yourself and your magic. Being offered an opportunity is most likely part of your manifestation process—it is an action step for you.

Sometimes, people try to rush the process. Their manifestation is coming, but they're feeling impatient. Persistence is key. Engage with the various strategies, spells, and richuals that are available to assist you! Perhaps there are things you need to learn first before you can handle all the money you're manifesting. Are you prioritizing your wealth witchery practice? Are you showing up every day, even if it's only for a few minutes? Most importantly, are you showing up every day as the version of yourself that already has what you most desire? As I have said many times in this book, it does you no good to do magic for ten minutes in the morning and then revert back to your old habits and thoughts for the rest of the day. You need to be the person that you want to be. Keep taking action and choosing what the rich witch version of yourself would choose. That is how you will manifest what you want consistently.

If you do happen to drop back into old ways of being, that's all right. Most of us do from time to time. Remember that you now have the tools to remove blockages and get back on track to achieving your rich witch life. Most of all, continue to trust that the Universe has your back. You are being taken care of, always! Stay magical, and know that because you have read this book and applied its teachings, infinite possibilities and abundant miracles are on their way to you, and your life is going to change now!

CONCLUSION

Hey, rich witch! Congratulations on starting your wealth witchery journey! I am so honored that you picked up this book to create your very best life. Know you can have anything you desire as long as you truly believe it. Embody the version of yourself that already has what you want. Everything you desire—or something better— is meant to be yours, because desire is your soul speaking to you. If you want Gucci loafers, you've got them. If you want a baby pink BMW with white leather seats, you've got it. If you want to write a book, you've got it. If you want to build a seven-figure business, you've got it. It's all about your vibe and the frequency you are attuned to.

When you change your energy, you change your life. Remember that manifesting is your birthright. If you focus on the magic and the energy of abundance, I know you will quickly manifest the amazing, beautiful life that you currently dream of having. Abundance is not only about money; it's about being joyful and wealthy in all areas of your life. When you are taken care of financially, you will be able to allow yourself to explore your magic and evolve on your spiritual path by creating the space and time for these practices.

If you want more magic and even more wealth recalibration, then come hang out with me on Instagram @pamelaunicorn. I'm always posting new money manifestation techniques and tools.

Thank you for allowing me to initiate you into the tradition of wealth witchery. I will see you soon. You can manifest anything you desire, even your dreamiest, richest life. Let's all rise together.

XO,

Pamela